SILENT FILMS IN ST. AUGUSTINE

UNIVERSITY PRESS OF FLORIDA

Florida A&M University, Tallahassee
Florida Atlantic University, Boca Raton
Florida Gulf Coast University, Ft. Myers
Florida International University, Miami
Florida State University, Tallahassee
New College of Florida, Sarasota
University of Central Florida, Orlando
University of Florida, Gainesville
University of North Florida, Jacksonville
University of South Florida, Tampa
University of West Florida, Pensacola

Rudolph Valentino by the fountain in the courtyard of the Hotel Ponce de Leon. (Courtesy of Donna L. Hill)

SILENT FILMS IN ST. AUGUSTINE

THOMAS GRAHAM

Foreword by Donna L. Hill

University Press of Florida

Gainesville · Tallahassee · Tampa · Boca Raton

Pensacola · Orlando · Miami · Jacksonville · Ft. Myers · Sarasota

This book may be available in an electronic edition.

22 21 20 19 18 17   6 5 4 3 2 1

Library of Congress Control Number: 2017933004
ISBN 978-0-8130-5453-7 (cloth)

The University Press of Florida is the scholarly publishing agency for the State University
System of Florida, comprising Florida A&M University, Florida Atlantic University, Florida
Gulf Coast University, Florida International University, Florida State University, New
College of Florida, University of Central Florida, University of Florida, University of North
Florida, University of South Florida, and University of West Florida.

University Press of Florida
15 Northwest 15th Street
Gainesville, FL 32611-2079
http://upress.ufl.edu

CONTENTS

FOREWORD

When most people think of the film capital of the world, it is natural that Hollywood, California, comes to mind. That city was listed proudly in the end credits in thousands of films and later countless television programs: "Filmed in Hollywood, CA." What most people do not remember is that film production in the United States really began on the east coast, in New York and New Jersey. It was largely the temperate climate, ample sunshine, and distance from the patents trust that led people to a small town called Hollywood to make films in the silent days. As time passed Hollywood grew to be synonymous with movies.

Film history could have been different; as this book relates, the cinematic capital could have gone in another direction entirely: St. Augustine, Florida. As we learn here, St. Augustine's film pedigree predates that of Hollywood by four years, starting in 1906. Sadly, the boom period for filmmaking in St. Augustine did not last long, yet many important names traveled to Florida to shoot films, beginning with early pioneers William Selig and the Kalem, Vitagraph, Edison, and Thanhouser Companies. Famous stars such as Pearl White, Crane Wilbur, Sidney Drew, Edith Storey (in the marvelous gender-bending *A Florida Enchantment* from 1914), Mary Garden, Billy Burke, Alla Nazimova, and vamp Theda Bara all made films in St. Augustine. Even the scandalous Evelyn Nesbitt took a turn before the cameras there.

Naturally, my interest in St. Augustine as a film locale is because Rudolph Valentino traveled to Florida to make the film *Stolen Moments*. It was filmed, in part, at the Hotel Ponce de Leon (now Flagler College). This was one of the last films where he was typed as a suave continental villain before he shot to fame as Julio Desnoyers in *The Four Horsemen of the Apocalypse*.

Dr. Graham's book reveals an important untold chapter of cinema history, one that I am eternally grateful has been written.

Donna L. Hill
author of *Rudolph Valentino, The Silent Idol*

FIRST EXPOSURES

1906–1911

St. Augustine is the oldest European city in the continental United States. Juan Ponce de León may have landed somewhere nearby in the year 1513 when he named the newly discovered land La Florida. In 1565 Pedro Menéndez de Avilés established a permanent settlement at St. Augustine, and in the following centuries the Spaniards, Indians, French, and English struggled for possession of the land, until it became part of the United States in 1821.

As early as the 1820s Americans living in northern states began coming to St. Augustine in the wintertime to escape frigid weather. These Yankee sojourners discovered an antique Spanish town, with stone houses whose balconies extended over narrow sandy streets, set amid a semitropical landscape bordering on the white sand beaches leading to the Atlantic Ocean. The gray stone Castillo de San Marcos, renamed Fort Marion by the United States, stood as an impressive monument to the military conflicts that had been fought for ownership of the town.

In the 1880s Henry M. Flagler, cofounder of Standard Oil Company with John D. Rockefeller, came to St. Augustine and constructed impressive, solid concrete resort hotels that looked like Spanish Renaissance palaces. His architects, Thomas Hastings and John Carrère, had started their careers at McKim, Mead & White—Stanford White was infamous as a bon vivant of New York society. Flagler also built a railroad that

The Vedder House was one of the old Spanish stone buildings that made St. Augustine so attractive to moviemakers. The Edison Company set *A Night at the Inn* there shortly before fire leveled the building along with several blocks of the city. (Courtesy of St. Augustine Historical Society)

connected Florida to the northern states and eventually extended south all the way to Key West. It was during the Flagler era that moviemaking companies discovered St. Augustine, and for a few years they used the Ancient City as the setting for films requiring a tropical or exotic atmosphere. Eventually, more than 120 films would be made partially or wholly in St. Augustine.

Thomas Edison, whose company supplied the electric dynamos for Flagler's hotels, may not have invented the moving picture, but his primitive motion picture device was the first to capture the public's imagination and make movies a commercial product. His "kinetoscope" consisted of a wooden box, two feet by three feet, with a slit in the top through which the viewer squinted. When the customer dropped a nickel in the change slot, a forty-foot strip of film rolled across a light projector, giving a thirty-second glimpse of animation. Albert E. Smith, a film pioneer with the Vitagraph Company, recalled, "No furor in entertainment history can compare with that aroused by Tom Edison's peep show. . . . Public excitement over the wooden cabinet with a slot at the top and a few moving pictures was unbelievable. It stirred controversy in scientific circles."[1]

Soon moving pictures were being projected onto screens, and large audiences of men, women, and children could watch a man chop down a tree, a sailboat glide across a pond, a woman push a baby stroller—anything that moved in an interesting way. These one-minute "flickers" simply catered to the public's astonishment that pictures could be made to move. By 1903 this novelty had worn off, and moviemakers started giving people films that told stories, most famously an eleven-minute thriller called *The Great Train Robbery*.

Within a matter of a few years the cameras that recorded pictures on film improved, and the projectors that showed the films operated more smoothly, eliminating the flicker of the first moving pictures. Lenses captured images with remarkable clarity, even by modern standards. By 1907 the citizens of cities across the land could walk into theaters and watch motion pictures playing almost continuously all afternoon and evening. As many as two million people a day took time to sit in the dark and be entertained. Motion picture companies churned out thousands of half-reel and one-reel animated stories lasting from as few as five minutes up to fifteen minutes.

St. Augustine residents were introduced to the movies with *The Corbett-Fitzsimmons Fight*, the longest moving picture made up to that point. It recorded the fourteen-round world heavyweight championship bout between Jim Corbett and Bob Fitzsimmons that took place in March of

Henry M. Flagler, an early partner in Standard Oil Company, built the Hotel Ponce de Leon (*pictured*) and several other large structures in Spanish Renaissance style. These were often used as the backdrops for scenes set in a variety of exotic locales, such as Italy, France, or Spain. (Courtesy of Flagler College Archives)

Actors and film crews sometimes made Flagler's Hotel Alcazar their headquarters because of its informal atmosphere and the amusements housed under its roof. (Courtesy of St. Augustine Historical Society)

1897. Veriscope's groundbreaking film created a sensation as it toured the country, finally arriving in St. Augustine in January 1898. The cavernous casino of Flagler's Hotel Alcazar served as the theater. Workmen stretched a canvas across one end of the large swimming pool, and spectators took seats on both sides of the surrounding mezzanine, an area where dances and bazaars were frequently staged. At first the projector operator wrestled with a balky machine, but eventually the crowd was treated to a very satisfactory exhibition.[2]

Two weeks later when the editor of St. Augustine's winter-season high-society magazine, *The Tatler*, witnessed the next moving picture presentation in the casino, featuring films produced by the Biograph Company, she was flabbergasted. The editor hardly knew what to make of the films. She dubbed the experience "one of the marvels of this electronic age. . . . This reproduction of living, moving men and women, life size, of galloping horses, dashing trains, gave very general satisfaction. . . . The enthusiasm was boundless. While the audience was a good one, had the people of St. Augustine had the least idea of what the show would be, the great hall would have been crowded."[3]

In succeeding years the casino would occasionally host films shown for the winter visitors to St. Augustine. In 1906 *The Tatler* advised its readers: "Next Monday moving pictures will be the attraction and no one should miss seeing them, as they are the best shown here and are equal to any exhibition anywhere. Admission twenty-five cents, and ten new subjects direct from New York will be given."[4]

The first place in St. Augustine to show moving pictures on a fairly regular basis was Genovar's Opera House on North St. George Street in the heart of town. The opera house had been constructed by family patriarch Bartolomé Genovar shortly after the Civil War, and all sorts of entertainments had been staged there over the years. The aging black abolitionist Frederick Douglass spoke to a mixed-race audience there in 1889 (and received a standing ovation), while on another occasion comic actor Joseph Jefferson performed *Rip Van Winkle*, a play he wrote that became his hallmark. By 1907 Genovar's was occasionally showing films such as *The Lighthouse Robbery*, a stage play that had been turned into a moving picture.[5]

In 1908 the Genovar brothers, William P. and Frank, entered the movie business in a serious way. First, they staged a free exhibition of films in the dance pavilion at St. Augustine Beach, then they opened Genovar's Electric Theater in a rented retail space near the family opera house on St. George Street.[6] Their first advertisement described the theater as "New, Bright, Cool." The last descriptor was important for a southern town in the midst of summer swelter. They offered a one-reel visual record of the Bill Squires–Tommy Burns heavyweight championship fight, a few "amusing" films, and some "scenes in other lands."[7]

At the same time as the Genovars were getting into the moving picture business full time, Gus Hooks opened the Plaza Theater in the Plaza Hotel on the corner of King Street and Hospital (today's Aviles) Street, on the south side of the old Spanish plaza. He advertised "the coolest theater in town," and staged matinee and evening showings every day except Sunday. Like the Genovars, he charged five cents admission for children and ten cents for adults. Shows did not always go smoothly. A September showing of the Kalem Company's *Ben Hur* came to an abrupt end when

The Orpheum Theatre operated in a converted retail store facing the central plaza. (Courtesy of St. Augustine Historical Society)

something burned out in the projection machine. Hooks held the film over until the next night, when a standing-room crowd watched the whole fifteen-minute epic.[8] Showing the same film two nights in a row was unusual in a time when films were exhibited once then packed off on a train for shipment to the movie house in the next town.

Shortly thereafter the Plaza Theater closed for major renovations. When it reopened in November, at the start of the winter tourist season, E. R. Groff took over management, and he boasted that the venue's new "motion picture machine" eliminated the flicker common to older machines. The premiere film in the new theater was Pathé's *Life and Passion of the Christ,* a hand-tinted color film that reigned for years as the most popular motion picture in America. The Plaza ran it for three nights.[9]

In the summer of 1909 the Genovar brothers moved their theater into a former retail space on the north side of the plaza, opposite the Plaza Theater. Renaming their venue the Orpheum, the Genovars built a stage at the front for plays and vaudeville, added banked seating, and installed fans to bring in fresh air. Their opening performance featured a live soloist and five film shorts.[10]

Two years earlier, in the summer of 1907, a group of investors that included some of the most prominent men in town had announced the formation of the Realty and Theater Company for the purpose of erecting a substantial brick building that could house both businesses and a large, modern theater for stage plays. This group aimed at displacing the outdated Genovar's Opera House. A. M. Taylor, one of the promoters of the new theater and a former manager of Flagler's Alcazar Casino, approached the sons of Joseph Jefferson to ask if the new theater could be named for their deceased father. The elder Jefferson had been a close friend of Henry Flagler's, and the sons readily agreed to the name.[11]

The Jefferson, which could seat about eight hundred people, stood on the corner of Cathedral Place and Cordova Street, next to Flagler's palatial Hotel Ponce de Leon, facing the same central plaza as the Orpheum and Plaza theaters. Being specifically designed as a theater, it had an advantage over the two earlier theaters, which operated in converted store spaces. However, the Jefferson aspired to be a high-class theater for respectable stage plays, not a movie house, and it showed movies only when traveling companies of actors were not booked for its stage. In September of 1909

The Jefferson Theatre gave St. Augustine a first-rate venue for live theater as well as motion pictures. To attract attention when the movie *Quo Vadis* was showing, the theater managers hired a circus wagon with lions to park outside. (From *Motion Picture News*)

William Jefferson and Joseph Jefferson Jr. performed *The Henrietta,* a comedy that their father, the theater's namesake, would have appreciated.[12]

Thus, by 1909 the people of St. Augustine, a town of about six thousand souls, enjoyed three theaters that competed for their patronage. During the hot summer months the town's population shrank as not only winter visitors but even some of the permanent residents moved north in search of respite from the heat. During this dull period the theaters (and churches too) often simply closed down for several months until the return of cool weather brought northern visitors and renewed energy for the winter season.

It was cold weather in the Northeast that brought moviemakers to Florida. At the time most motion picture companies were headquartered in New York City; across the Hudson River in Fort Lee, New Jersey; in Philadelphia; or in Chicago. Almost all filming was done outside in natural light because of the primitive state of electric lighting. "Indoor" scenes were performed in front of a one- or two-wall outdoor backdrop that simulated the interior of a room. Often a canopy of muslin cloth would be suspended over the stage to filter the sunlight and eliminate shadows. Later, companies erected glass greenhouse studios for protection from the elements. Each year when December arrived the movie men and women saw the sunlight fading and temperatures dropping. The low humidity of cold air created a particular problem for the cameramen, since the moving parts in the machinery sparked static electricity that created spidery white streaks across the film.

Warm, sunny, humid Florida beckoned from just thirty-two hours away by train. The logic of relocating to a Florida venue for the dead-of-winter months was inescapable, and Jacksonville provided a medium-sized city with all the amenities requisite for movie production. Exposed film could be shipped back north for processing and editing. Just another hour south of Jacksonville stood St. Augustine, America's Ancient City.

The first film known to have been made in St. Augustine was a ten-minute travelogue entitled *A Trip to St. Augustine,* released by the Selig Polyscope Company of Chicago in June of 1906. St. Augustine's unique Spanish architecture would prove an irresistible draw for makers of documentary films in following years, but soon it would also attract makers of photoplays that required out-of-the-ordinary settings. The first such

When the Pathé company set up shop at the Fountain of Youth, they built this out-door stage to shoot "interior" scenes under natural light. The thin fabric canopy could be drawn over the stage to reduce the sharp shadows cast by strong sunlight. (Courtesy of St. Augustine Historical Society)

company of moviemakers would arrive a little more than two years later. In succeeding years St. Augustine's old Spanish structures, Flagler's magnificent hotels, and the area's semitropical landscape would stand in for Spain, Italy, France, Brazil, Egypt, Arabia, South Africa, Hawaii, and even California.

During the waning days of 1908 a troupe of players from the Kalem Company arrived in Florida from New York. Kalem had been founded just a year earlier. Their business office stood in Manhattan but, lacking a proper studio, the intrepid film pioneers specialized in shooting on location. Soon they would travel to Ireland and to Palestine in search of unusual scenery, but first they came to Florida. The Kalem group set up headquarters for the season in a suburb of Jacksonville at the Roseland Hotel, a modest frame house with verandas on three sides where guests could enjoy the sun and warmth. A wooden stage erected in the yard served as a studio, and various outdoor settings provided backdrops for

The great man himself, Henry M. Flagler, attended the Ponce de Leon Celebration in 1909. He is preceded by his chauffeur and is accompanied by Mrs. James Ingraham, wife of one of his chief lieutenants. (Courtesy of P. K. Yonge Library of Florida History, University of Florida)

the one-reel action movies the company created at a furious pace—sometimes two in a week.[13]

On one occasion the Kalem actors took the train from Jacksonville to St. Augustine to film a scene at old Fort Marion for the one-reel short *The Seminole's Vengeance* (1909). The action film portrayed a famous incident in the Second Seminole War when the Seminole chief Coacoochee escaped from imprisonment in the fort and returned to battle. At this time motion picture companies did not give credit to any of the principals involved in films, but it is highly likely that Sidney Olcott directed and acted in the movie, while Gene Gauntier wrote the scenario and played a female lead—as the pair had earlier for *Ben Hur*. As time went on and the public came to recognize Gauntier's face, she became known as "The Kalem Girl." Gauntier would go on to become one of the most prolific screenwriters of the silent era.[14]

On April 1, 1909, the Kalem cameras were back in action at Fort Marion to record the landing of the Spanish explorer Juan Ponce de León in St.

Augustine's reenactment of the discovery of Florida in 1513. The roles of Spaniards and Indians were played by local men and boys who had been given three days off to take part in the Ponce de Leon Celebration. The whole town turned out for thrilling battles on the fort green, a parade through the streets of the town, military drills by visiting militia from Georgia, powerboat races on the bay, and a grand ball in the evening. Kalem produced two separate versions of *The Ponce de Leon Fete*, and in May Genovar's Opera House and the Plaza Theater staged dueling screenings of the films. During the showings, the audiences kept up running commentaries as various familiar faces from the community flashed onto the screen.[15] The film enjoyed a national release and would be repeated locally from time to time in future years.

In January 1910, a party from the Lubin Company stopped by St. Augustine's venerable Florida House hotel for two days to shoot some scenes for a movie entitled *A Honeymoon Through Snow to Sunshine*. The storyline follows a couple of newlyweds from wintery Philadelphia (Lubin's home city) to Jacksonville, St. Augustine, Palm Beach, and Miami. According to the review in *Moving Picture World,* while in St. Augustine the couple "stop at the famous Ponce de Leon, the courtyard of which is the most remarkable bit of architecture, and they also inspect Fort Marion."[16] On arriving in Miami, the bride kisses a strange man, angering the groom, but the bride is only teasing since the stranger is her brother.[17] The director of this simple short film was Arthur Hotaling, one of Lubin's most prolific filmmakers, who would introduce Oliver Hardy to the public in the 1914 film *Outwitting Daddy*, shot in Jacksonville.[18]

Lubin rushed to get *A Honeymoon Through Snow to Sunshine* into theaters, and it reached St. Augustine just two months after it had been filmed. Of course, local people were excited to see their hometown in the movies. "Never in its history," reported the *St. Augustine Record,* "was the capacity of the Plaza theater tested as it was all day yesterday."[19]

The Kalem players were back in Jacksonville in the winter of 1911, and they came to St. Augustine to film *In Old Florida*, a conventional love story set in Spanish times. Olcott and Gauntier again collaborated on this movie. A Spanish girl falls in love with an American visitor, but her father disapproves and favors a local man. The lovers manage to elude the father and reach a priest, who marries them. Most of the scenes were shot

Tom Mix, later to gain fame as a movie cowboy, appeared in *The Rose of Old St. Augustine* as a Seminole warrior. Mix is probably the large-nosed Indian standing in the right foreground. (From *Cyclopedia of Motion-Picture Work*, vol. 2)

on the landscaped grounds of Flagler's Hotel Ponce de Leon. The movie magazine *Motography* declared, "The settings are good and the historical atmosphere pleasing." This would become the unanimous judgment of later reviewers of St. Augustine–made motion pictures: the picturesque old town photographed well.[20]

Selig Polyscope followed Kalem to St. Augustine a short time later to shoot *The Rose of Old St. Augustine* (1911), another tale set in Spanish Florida, but this time a love story intertwined with lots of action and adventure. A French privateer and a Spanish soldier vie for the affections of a Spanish girl. Since the narrative required a large cast of pirates, soldiers, and Indians, many local men and women were hired as "supers" to take part in the action. The most noted actor in the film played only a supporting role: Tom Mix appeared as Black Hawk, a Seminole warrior. It would not be until later in the decade that Mix would rise to become the most famous of the cowboy actors. He enjoyed the advantage of actually being a real cowboy who happened to work his way into Westerns in small roles and emerged as a star because he really could ride and rope and perform his own stunts. One of his leading ladies in later movies was

Louella Modie Maxam, who had been born in St. Augustine but left with her family for California when she was a young child.[21]

The Rose of Old St. Augustine, though only a one-reel "short," attracted a lot of attention in the movie world and turned a spotlight on St. Augustine as a place to make movies. *Moving Picture World* asserted, "This is an unusually romantic story and an exciting one. It is well acted, especially on the heroine's part, and though there is a little sawing of the air and theatrical posing in the picture, on the whole it maintains just the right atmosphere to give a delightful effect. . . . The Selig Company has evidently spared no expense in making this picture."[22] Actually, it was not necessary to build any expensive sets for the picture: the actors simply had to play their roles against the backdrops of Anastasia Island sand dunes, the stone piers of the City Gates, and the ramparts and dungeons of Fort Marion.

Motography seconded the opinion of *Moving Picture World*, describing *The Rose* as "a romantic historical drama of large proportions, presented with strong dramatic effect and much art in the pictorial features. . . . It is all in all one of the most satisfactory historical films ever made in this country."[23] High praise for a film made in a (then) remote corner of America.

At this early point in motion picture history, St. Augustine's experience paralleled that of the whole industry: It started with pictures of interesting Florida sites and progressed to films that used drama and action to tell a story—one that could be completed in a fifteen-minute reel of celluloid.

2

THE THANHOUSER SEASON

1912

In 1913 Epes Winthrop Sargent wrote a pioneering book, *Techniques of the Photoplay,* that included an account of how St. Augustine's unique architecture brought an unnamed film production company to town: "One director knew of a hotel built in the Arabian style. He did not wait for Arabian stories to come in. He had the place photographed from several angles and sent these to an author with a request for three plays to fit these settings. When the stories were completed the photographs were returned, and by a system of markings each scene was written to fit the whole or some part of the places shown in the photographs."[1]

Given that the book was published in 1913 there is only one director who fits this description: George O. Nichols of the Thanhouser Company. Or perhaps the man in question was Edwin Thanhouser himself. These men and a company of players spent six weeks in St. Augustine in the winter of 1912 and produced seventeen movies, two of which were pure "Arabians." At the time the Thanhouser Company was advertising that it would produce two films a week for distribution companies and theaters. It surpassed that goal, managing to create almost three one-reel shorts per week during the days in St. Augustine.

Earlier in January the Thanhouser troupe had departed from their New Rochelle, New York, headquarters, heading to the docks of New

York City to board the Clyde steamship *Apache*, which made regular runs between New York and Florida during the winter season. During the voyage south they recorded some scenes on deck to be used in the movies they planned to make. Arriving in St. Augustine by train from the Clyde Line's port in Jacksonville on January 13, the Thanhouser troupe checked into the Granada Hotel. The Granada was a relatively modest wood-and-stucco building located between Flagler's huge hotels Ponce de Leon and Alcazar.

Edwin Thanhouser was accompanied by his wife, Gertrude, and his two children, while Nichols brought his wife and son with him. Actor James Cruze came with his sister, May Boser Cruze, and actor Joseph Graybill's wife came along as well. The families must have considered the trip to sunny Florida a working vacation. The rest of the party included many regulars from Thanhouser productions, including William Russell, Florence La Badie, Marguerite Snow, and Viola Alberti. They dubbed St. Augustine the "Southern Company Headquarters."[2]

The moviemakers did not have to travel far to start filming. Right next door to the Granada stood the Zorayda Club, a restaurant occupying a Moorish villa built thirty years earlier by the eccentric Boston world traveler and amateur architect Franklin W. Smith. The Villa Zorayda had been one of the first buildings constructed in the United States using cast-in-place concrete. Smith molded the concrete into arabesque patterns inspired by Spain's Alhambra. The building showed well in Thanhouser's first production, *The Arab's Bride*, starring Florence La Badie, James Cruze, and William Russell. The sand dunes of St. Augustine's beach stood in for the Sahara. *Moving Picture World* approved: "This first picture by them abounds in gorgeous, accurate settings."[3]

Production of the next release, *For Sale—A Life*, had actually begun earlier on the *Apache* when Joseph Graybill had been filmed as an invalid dying of tuberculosis, accompanied to the warmth of Florida by his beautiful wife, Marguerite Snow. The couple meet a handsome "clubman," James Cruze, at a hotel (the Alcazar), and when Graybill's character realizes that the clubman is attracted to his wife, he offers to sell her for $10,000 and obtain a divorce. Thus, she would be relieved of caring for a dying husband and could move forward with a new love. When the wife

Franklin W. Smith built a Moorish fantasy palace, the Villa Zorayda, as his winter home in St. Augustine. The inner patio was covered by a glass roof, making it feasible to shoot film inside. (Courtesy of St. Augustine Historical Society)

Florence La Badie and William Russell, dressed for *The Arab's Bride*, look comfortably at home in Franklin Smith's exotically decorated Villa Zorayda. (From *Moving Picture News*)

learns of the proposal she rejects it. Her husband soon succumbs to his disease, leaving her with the possibility of a new life with the clubman, but the ending is left up to the audience's imagination.[4]

Another motion picture made that winter took advantage of a different iconic Florida locale, an orange grove. At the time St. Augustine had many orange groves close by the city, and Garnett Grove, a noted tourist attraction located just outside town, may have been the setting for *The Girl of the Grove*. After he returned to New York, Thanhouser explained: "Perhaps our Florida pictures' biggest bid for popularity was on their unusual settings, the locations and backgrounds that St. Augustine and thereabouts can boast." Another scene featuring another Florida icon, an alligator, ended up on the cutting room floor. Thanhouser's children later remembered that a baby alligator was filmed eating hamburger, and this footage was intended to be used in an action movie where a large alligator ate a man. However, the image was deemed too gruesome to be used in a release.[5]

St. Augustine's populace was delighted and intrigued that famous New York movie personalities were going through their paces in their midst. "The Spanish costumes attract much attention," reported a local newspaperman, "and crowds of interested spectators quickly gather about the camera when a photoplay is in progress." When a Thanhouser movie was shown at the Jefferson, the reporter wrote: "This is one of Thanhouser's newest and best subjects, made by the very company who are in the city at the present time, and when you see the pictures on Sunday you will know that the actors and actresses in the picture are sitting among you in the audience looking at themselves act."[6] Later in the spring, when the Thanhouser movies appeared in St. Augustine's theaters, local residents packed the houses to catch a glimpse of themselves and their neighbors in the movies.

Some of St. Augustine's wealthy leisure-class hotel patrons may have entertained themselves with roles in *The Saleslady*. Although St. Augustine had been supplanted by Palm Beach as the winter resort of choice for America's millionaires, the old town still retained a winter colony of the social elite. *The Saleslady* is the story of a department store employee who comes up with a novel idea for displaying the store's new fashion line of gowns and hats for ladies. Thanhouser advertised the movie as "The

Marguerite Snow, William Russell, and James Cruze form a romantic triangle atop Fort Marion in Thanhouser's *The Ring of a Spanish Grandee* (1912). (From *The Cinema*)

$40,000 Fashion Film," because a parade of women appear in the film in gorgeous apparel. *Moving Picture News* declared, "It is likely the most pretentious thing in the way of a 'fashion film' that has ever been attempted."[7]

Several St. Augustine landmarks received attention from filmmakers. The old Spanish *castillo*, now Fort Marion, remained under the control of the U.S. War Department, but essentially it served only as a tourist attraction. Its massive gray walls, expansive courtyard, and corner watchtowers supplied interesting backdrops to stories such as *A Love Long Ago* and *The Ring of a Spanish Grandee*. A short comedy, *The Golf Caddie's Dog,* was set on the four-hole golf course that circled the fort green. In this little romance, a clever black caddie boy saves the heroine from a "dude" who threatens to steal her away from the man that the caddie deems a worthier match. The caddie lathers up his dog's mouth with soap to simulate rabies then sets the dog on the "dude," who climbs a tree while the worthy young man rescues the girl.[8]

The most prominent landmark on St. Augustine's beach—the tall, black-and-white-striped lighthouse—figures as the location of *Rejuvenation*. In this tale a wealthy young man (James Cruze) drifts away in a small

rowboat and is rescued by the daughter of the lighthouse keeper (Florence La Badie). He spurns wealth to marry the daughter and live a simple
life. Years later when a friend from his past life recognizes him, the man
tells him that he has found a new, happier life on the seashore.[9]

All of the previous movies were one-reel shorts, except for *The Golf
Caddie's Dog* (which shared a reel with *The Taming of Mary*), and *Jess:
A Sister's Sacrifice* (which encompassed two reels). *Jess* was based on H.
Rider Haggard's popular novel set in South Africa at the time of the Boer
War. The two reels of this epic story would be released separately, a week
apart, as episode 1 and episodes 2 and 3. In these films St. Augustine filled
in for "the sun kissed sands of Africa."[10]

On February 29 a crowd of townsfolk gathered at the railway station to
bid farewell to the Thanhouser troupe. Their departure made front-page
news.[11] Three years would pass before they would return to St. Augustine.

In an ironic case of life imitating art, Joseph Graybill, the invalid of
For Sale—A Life, would die of spinal meningitis a year later in New York

Not all movies shot in St. Augustine took advantage of the grand architecture. William Russell, James Cruze, and Marguerite Snow stand in a farmyard in *Whom God
Hath Joined*. (Courtesy of Margaret Herrick Library)

City. James Cruze and Marguerite Snow, whose fate is left hanging at the conclusion of that film, would be married in real life in January 1913, about the time Graybill died. Cruze would go on to become one of the most highly paid directors in Hollywood. The first epic Western, *The Covered Wagon* (1923), featuring sweeping panoramas of mountains and deserts, advertised James Cruze as director but did not mention any of the actors in the drama.

3

MOVIES DISCOVER ST. AUGUSTINE

1913–1914

By 1913 movie actors and actresses no longer performed anonymously. The public had come to recognize certain personalities they saw on screen and wanted to know just who they were. Production companies realized that they could more effectively market films if they publicized the names and faces of their players. Movie fan magazines appeared and gave birth to the "movie star." Young people collected trading cards with photos of their favorite actors. Male audiences came to the movies to appreciate the faces and forms of the actresses, while female patrons admired their stylish dresses—and the handsome male leads as well.

LUBIN

During the winter of 1913 a band of "gypsy" moviemakers from Lubin, the company that had produced the pioneering Florida film *Honeymoon Through Snow to Sunshine* three years earlier, came south and set up shop at the old Florida Yacht Club building in the Riverside neighborhood of Jacksonville. The actors and technicians lived comfortably in rented homes near a building that had been transformed into a fully equipped studio facility.

George Nichols, who had been a director for Thanhouser in St. Augustine the previous winter, brought a few of the Lubin crew to St. Augustine.

Ormi Hawley does not look pleased at being sold into slavery in this scene from *Women of the Desert*, Lubin's 1913 film shot in the courtyard of Fort Marion. (From *Motography*)

Ormi Hawley, Earl Metcalfe, Marguerite Ne Moyer, Irving White, and Edwin Carewe made *The First Prize* using the town as a setting. One reviewer dismissed the story as a simple romance, but still praised the "lovely views of Florida in the background."[1]

Nichols' next film exploited St. Augustine's assets to the maximum. Scenes for *Women of the Desert* were taken on the beach, at the Villa Zorayda, on the grounds of the Hotel Ponce de Leon, and in Fort Marion. *Moving Picture World* gave it a strong review: "This love story of the Sahara was taken in Florida and makes a very fair offering, chiefly because the Lubin company was able to find backgrounds that give a suggestion of reality to its desert scenes, where the Arab tents are pitched and also of the Moorish town, the palace of the Caliph, where the bedouin hero finds and rescues the heroine sold into slavery by her jealous sister."[2]

When *Women of the Desert* appeared at the Orpheum a few months later, the *St. Augustine Record* recommended it to townspeople, saying, "This picture is an elaborate one and is scattered over many places in the many scenes. The beach, the fort, the streets and big hotels of St.

Augustine are utilized in getting the requisite scenes. It is a magnificent play, but its local flavor will make it doubly interesting here."[3]

ÉCLAIR

In March fourteen members of the American Éclair Company checked into the Hotel Alcazar to spend some time shooting scenes for *Sons of a Soldier,* the most ambitious film made locally to that date.[4] This three-reel epic follows the exploits of the Primrose family from the Revolutionary War through the Civil War to a hypothetical future war with Japan. The reviewer for *Moving Picture News* thought that the film would force the country "at last to face the growing peril of the Far East." In this story about a family of illustrious patriotic warriors, two brothers become involved in the conflict with Japan. The younger brother, portrayed by Jack W. Johnston, becomes an officer on the front lines against the invaders, while the other, played by Frederick Truesdale, is elected president of the United States. Truesdale bore a resemblance to Woodrow Wilson, a possible candidate for president at the time the movie was made. Barbara Tennant plays the love interest in the story and is able in the last reel to save the younger brother, who has been falsely accused of desertion.[5]

A local man, Joe Copps, only a boy at the time, years later recalled that Barbara Tennant had been his "first love." He explained she was "a hot gal in those days." He added that Éclair had used the Casa Cola Ranch north of town as the setting for the movie.[6]

UNIVERSAL FILMS

The year 1913 happened to be the four hundredth anniversary of Juan Ponce de León's discovery of Florida, and St. Augustine again staged a three-day extravaganza. Universal Films used two reels of film to record the revelry and rushed a copy to the Jefferson Theatre just a few days after the event. The town's citizenry packed the theater for two nights in a row to see themselves on the screen.[7] The picture was subsequently sent around the state of Florida, but it evidently did not have a national release.

The Ponce de Leon Celebration had been staged by the leaders of St. Augustine's business community as a way of encouraging winter-season tourists to linger in town for a few days longer. As was true for almost every American city, local boosters constantly sought ways to promote the economy by bringing in outsiders and their money. Since movie companies brought people to town who spent money in hotels, restaurants, and various other businesses, the Chamber of Commerce and local government officials attempted to entice the movie people to locate more permanently in St. Augustine, where they could take advantage of the city's unique attractions. Moviemaking might even become an established local enterprise.

Their efforts paid off in the winter season of 1913–1914. After a long, sultry summer of economic lethargy, the return of cooler weather in October brought a new wave of motion picture production crews to Florida, and one of the biggest located itself in the Ancient City.

PATHÉ

The French-based company Pathé Frères, one of the oldest of the motion picture makers, operated a chain of theaters in Europe and maintained a studio in Fort Lee, New Jersey. Pathé took a six-month lease on a portion of the tract then called Neptune Park, which was located just on the northern outskirts of town. This property had long been a garden spot favored by winter visitors. An original character, Luella Day McConnell, fresh from the goldfields of the Yukon, had recently purchased it.[8]

Northern visitors were intrigued by a story that had already become accepted as "tradition," even though it was of fairly recent origin: A writer for *Motion Picture News* reported, "The new Pathé outdoor studio in St. Augustine is distinguished by at least one unique feature. On the grounds of the property is located a spring, which tradition in the old Spanish city states is the spring visited by Ponce de Leon in his search for the fountain of perpetual youth, and which for some time he took to be the object of his search. For years the former owners of the spring charged admission to this spring because of the tradition."[9] (Ironically, although Juan Ponce de León almost certainly never came to the spot, it is very probably the site of Pedro Menéndez de Avilés' original settlement of St. Augustine.)

First on the scene at Neptune Park was the menagerie of wild animals Pathé had arranged to play roles in some of the movies planned for

Paul Bourgeois' two camels from the Pathé menagerie pose with a tourist inside Fort Marion. The entry to the fort's chapel remained in a state of ruin at the time the movie was made. (Courtesy of Castillo de San Marcos Archives, National Park Service)

production. A Frenchman, Paul Bourgeois, owned the animals and for several years had worked with Pathé in France and then at Fort Lee. He came to St. Augustine with seven train carloads of animals: two elephants, two camels, two ostriches, ten lions, two tigers, a leopard, and an eighteen-foot python. In an interview given earlier at Fort Lee, Bourgeois said of the big cats, "Oh, they are not as dangerous as they look." He explained that Princess, the tigress, was a veteran actor. He asserted that firmness, kindness, and patience could make a lion "as gentle as a tabby cat."[10]

Something must have happened to the animals on the train ride to Florida, for by the time the lions and tigers reached the walled compound that had been erected for them at Neptune Park, they had become "wild denizens of the jungles of Africa and Asia. . . . They [were as] treacherous and as fierce as the day they were torn from their native haunts." Citizens of St. Augustine were invited to come and watch the animals being fed at four in the afternoon and see them go through their paces in the large

Nell Craig poses with a tiger skin on the Pathé outdoor stage. This photo was shot while she was playing an Indian woman in *Pearl of the Punjab*. (Courtesy of St. Augustine Historical Society)

iron-caged arena. The animals were only part of a carnival that included games, food, and various other amusements. On Thursday evenings a band would play for dancing.[11]

Frederick E. Wright, one of Pathé's lead directors, headed the company in St. Augustine. The first film undertaken, *Bungling Bink's Bunco*, employed two leading actors—Walter Seymour and Lillian Wiggins—and several of the large cats. In the play Seymour tries to impress his girlfriend, Wiggins, by having himself photographed next to a stuffed lion and telling her of his prowess as a great hunter. Unfortunately for Seymour, his intended insists on going to Africa to see him in action. In the film, as the couple receives a big send-off from the railroad station, the name "St. Augustine City Band" could be spotted by sharp-eyed locals. All sorts of comedic action ensues in the three-reel movie. There were some real-life incidents as well. Prince, the large Bengal tiger, got carried away during the shooting of one scene, when Seymour tripped while running away, and Prince sank his claws into Seymour's hips. Trainers quickly wrestled Prince off and both man and tiger emerged from the affair without serious injury.[12]

Wright's next film was more ambitious. *Pearl of the Punjab* tackled the sensitive issue of interracial marriage. Walter Seymour, a British medical officer in India, quarrels with his fiancée, Lillian Wiggins, over her family's mistreatment of Wiggins' adopted Indian stepsister, played by Nell Craig. Subsequently believing that he has killed a man, Seymour runs away with Craig to her home village and later marries her. In the last reel, Wiggins' character crosses paths with Seymour and Craig in the wilds of India. Seymour turns down the chance to return to English society and remains with his Indian wife.

Nell Craig and an unidentified actor pose in front of the decorative iron fountain (not the supposed Fountain of Youth) that long stood on the grounds of the Fountain of Youth Park. The fountain is now gone, but the circle of stones that surrounded it survives. (Courtesy of St. Augustine Historical Society)

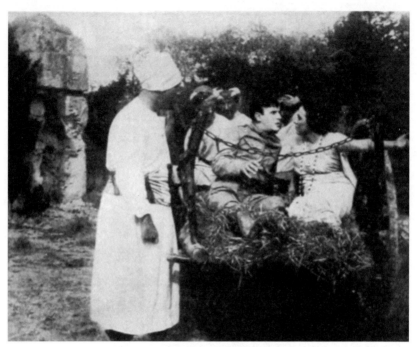

The Old Spanish Chimney, a landmark on Old Beach Road, offered an interesting setting for a scene from *Pearl of the Punjab*. (From *Motography*)

Director Wright extravagantly boasted to a Jacksonville newspaper reporter of his resourcefulness in exploiting local scenery: "In and around St. Augustine I found every location needed and an expert could not have told but what the pictures had been made in the old world—India, Egypt, Morocco, Persia—instead of the state of Florida." In regard to *Pearl of the Punjab* Wright explained:

> An old mill, perhaps erected by some Spaniard in the long ago, furnished me with the background for my leading woman to heroically save an English army officer from arrest and punishment. A ruin of an old shell chimney on Anastasia Island, with an oxcart and several Hindoos, gave an exact counterpart of a thoroughfare in the jungle that I had seen in India. A lodge on Lewis Point on the Sebastian river gave me a hunting lodge in the Central Provinces of Hindoostan. The residence of W. A. Knight became the mansion of a millionaire Englishman in Calcutta. A row of dilapidated old houses in the center of the

town, with the addition of elephants and camels, and I had a teeming thoroughfare in a jungle village.[13]

Wright's "old mill" was actually the modern Hood Mill on Riberia Street, which used a rustic-looking waterwheel driven by artesian well water. The coquina-stone Spanish well and chimney still stand on Old Beach Road, and the ox and cart were borrowed from a still photographer who used them as props in taking souvenir photos for tourists. The picnic pavilion at Lewis Point on Moultrie Creek served as the hunting lodge. The elephants evidently took a four-mile walk to get to the site. William A. Knight was a businessman from Zanesville, Ohio, who spent winters in St. Augustine with his family. Their substantial home, Three Oaks, located on Oneida Street overlooking the marshes, would be used in later movies as well. The "row of dilapidated old houses" stood along Hospital Street (today Aviles Street) and included the Fatio House, now a National Historic Landmark. The Florida East Coast Railway station also appeared in a scene. A reporter for the *St. Augustine Record* who watched the filming

The picnic pavilion at Lewis Point, south of town, became an Indian bungalow for *Pearl of the Punjab*. (From *Moving Picture World*)

noted, "A rajah, in all the glory of oriental attire, and a lady of his harem were conspicuous features in the picture."[14]

Motion picture making had already changed dramatically since the time just two years earlier when Thanhouser could crank out two or three movies in a week's time. During Pathé's three-month stay in St. Augustine, the troupe finished only three projects: some outdoor scenes for the short film *Good Pals*, which had been started in New Jersey; the three-reel *Bungling Bink's Bunco*; and *Pearl of the Punjab*, which ran to five reels. The day of the one-reel movie seemed to be passing from the scene. *Motion Picture News* ran a story in October of 1913 entitled "Is the Short Length Film Doomed?" This article concluded that the five-reel "feature film" would become the standard, and one-reel movies would survive only as comedy shorts shown as added attractions.[15]

Director Wright agreed: "The motion picture industry has grown even beyond the wildest dreams of its pioneers. The one reel picture was in vogue at first. It cost a few hundred dollars to produce. Today it costs $3,000 to $10,000 per reel. Five and eight reel movies cost $100,000."[16]

In early February the Pathé company started work on another film based on Hall Caine's novel *The Christian*; though this would be the working title, ultimately the picture would be released as *When Rome Ruled* (1914). The film stars Nell Craig as Nydia, a Christian girl, and Clifford Bruce as a pagan Roman nobleman named Caius, who falls in love with Nydia. Bourgeois' lions, as would be expected, threaten to devour Nydia, and Caius comes to the rescue in the nick of time. "This is undoubtedly resorting to melodramatic methods of the crudest sort," sniffed the critic for *Motion Picture News*, "but what difference does it make if the audience finds great joy in the sensation produced?" Reviewers praised the settings of the film for their realistic Roman provincial appearance, and the Christians-versus-lions scenes passed the believability test.[17]

Wright told a story about the filming that might be true. He said that the company looked for a lamb to be sacrificed to a lion, but after scouring the countryside, they could come up only with a full-grown ram. When placed in the arena with a lion, the ram butted the lion and chased him around the enclosure. A trial with a second lion resulted in the same outcome, and Wright gave up on the scene.[18]

Clifford Bruce poses as a proud Roman from *When Rome Ruled*. The large clay urn is one of several that can still be seen at Fountain of Youth Archaeological Park. Bruce would later play roles in *A Fool There Was* and other locally produced films. (Courtesy of St. Augustine Historical Society)

A group of players from *When Rome Ruled* pose next to the outer works of Fort Marion. (Courtesy of St. Augustine Historical Society)

When the movie played at the Orpheum later that summer, the audience judged it the best movie made so far in St. Augustine. The *St. Augustine Record* enthused, "It was in all details a St. Augustine picture. All the scenes were laid here, and the actors and actresses are all well known in the community, several of them being residents of the city."[19]

In February two more Pathé contingents arrived in town. The first, led by director Frank Powell, came with Eleanor Woodruff, Marguerite Risser, and Jack Standing to shoot just one scene at Three Oaks in order to complete a film (probably *All Love Excelling*) already nearly finished at the home studio in New Jersey. *Motography* magazine reported Powell had taken "the trip to Florida for the sake of a few meters of tropical backgrounds. Frank says realism is the thing and that's what he is after."[20]

The second team of players came for a more ambitious project. Directors Louis Gasnier and Donald McKenzie headed a group of twenty people. (Gasnier is best known today for his 1936 film *Reefer Madness*.) Some of Pathé's leading stars were in the company, including Pearl White, Crane Wilbur, Paul Panzer, and a lesser-known but veteran actor, Edward

José.[21] White attracted attention by checking into Flagler's upscale Hotel Alcazar while other members of the crew took rooms at the aging Florida House in the midst of the old Spanish part of town. Their project consisted of shooting scenes for a forthcoming twenty-episode serial entitled *The Perils of Pauline*, a rip-roaring adventure series that would make Pearl White a star and captivate the attention of audiences across America and Europe. In each episode Pauline encounters danger from some diverse array of circumstances, ranging from modern hazards, such as a crashing airplane, to historical threats, including pirates and savage Indians.

The first episode begins with Pauline (Pearl White) playing tennis with Harry Marvin (Crane Wilbur) on the tennis court of elderly and infirm millionaire Stanford Marvin, Harry's father and Pauline's guardian. (The Marvin estate is actually the Hotel Ponce de Leon.) Raymond Owen (Paul Panzer) emerges from the courtyard of the hotel to call them in for a meeting with Mr. Marvin. The old man explains that his will leaves half of his fortune to Harry and the other half to his ward, Pauline. Until

Crane Wilbur and Pearl White pause from their tennis game on the courts of the Hotel Ponce de Leon in an early scene from *The Perils of Pauline*. The courts have now been replaced by lawn. (From *Motography*)

Pauline marries, however, Stanford's personal secretary, Owen, will serve as executor of her estate; and if she dies, Owen will continue as executor indefinitely.[22] The elderly Mr. Marvin soon dies, and the rest of the serial hangs on the provision of the will regarding Pauline's inheritance. Owen tries repeatedly to bump off Pauline through ingenious though ultimately unsuccessful schemes. (Clifford Bruce appears as a gypsy leader in a later episode.) Through it all the intrepid but clueless Pauline fails to realize that Owen is out to get her. All the while Harry yearns to marry Pauline, but she is a modern woman who wants to experience adventures and write about them for magazines.

The two episodes shot in St. Augustine revolve around Pauline's desire to fly in an airplane. In preparation for shooting the scenes, Pathé's technicians erected sets designed to resemble airplane hangars at Lewis Park, St. Augustine's baseball field located at the south end of town on a marshy peninsula. A large sign reading "Great Aviation Meet" was nailed to the fence surrounding the ballpark, and everyone in town was invited

Crane Wilbur and Pearl White watch as an airplane crashes in episode 2 of *The Perils of Pauline*. The scene was shot at the baseball park in St. Augustine. Behind Wilbur and White in the stands are Francis Carlyle and Paul Panzer, the evil men who sabotaged the plane. (From *Motography*)

A group of actors poses outside the W. A. Knight home, which appears in a few scenes of *The Perils of Pauline*. A penciled note on the back of the photograph identifies the man on the left as Paul Panzer. Could the woman holding the puppy be Pearl White? (Courtesy of St. Augustine Historical Society)

to come and fill the stands for the production. George A. Gray, an aviator based in Jacksonville for the winter, flew his Wright pusher biplane down to play his role in the drama. Prior to the flying exhibition, Owen stealthily sabotages the airplane by partly severing a control wire of the aircraft so that it will snap in flight, causing the airplane to crash. Harry saves Pauline by draining gasoline from the tank of her car so that she stalls while driving to the airfield, consequently missing the flight. The road used for this scene was Lewis Point Road, which in reality lies miles away from the baseball park. (This was the same road down which the elephants had walked in *Pearl of the Punjab*.)[23]

When the movie appeared at the Orpheum, local folks could watch themselves in the stadium scene. *Motion Picture News* gave St. Augustine's amateur actors a rave review, noting that when the airplane crashes "a number of women, not members of the Pathé company, fainted in the filled grandstands, adding unconsciously to the vividness of the scene." Of course, no airplane actually crashed at the ballpark, and the crash sequence used in the film is not of Gray's Wright biplane.[24]

The Perils of Pauline was not the first serial, but it was the first to capture the public's imagination. Following its sensational popularity, the wholesome all-American girl Pearl White starred in more serials and adventure movies through the rest of the decade. In the 1920s her appeal as a female action heroine began to wane. When her health deteriorated, she retired from acting and moved to France, where she passed away in 1938. In 1947 Betty Hutton would portray White in a biographical film entitled *Perils of Pauline*. In this film Paul Panzer, the evil Owen of the 1914 serial, makes a brief cameo appearance as an elderly businessman.

Early in the morning of April 2, 1914, a fire broke out in the Florida House hotel, and the old hotel, dating to before the Civil War, went up in flames like a tinderbox, igniting buildings for blocks all around. Genovar's Opera House disappeared quickly. The colonial-era Vedder House crumbled into rubble. Many of the winter-season guests of the Florida House had recently checked out, but the Pathé people were still in their rooms. Most guests escaped with no more than the clothes on their backs, but a cameraman named Harrison grabbed his camera and started grinding away to capture images of the fire lighting up the night sky. Pathé would use the footage in its Weekly News reel, reporting that half of St. Augustine burned.[25]

As the winter season came to an end, rumors swirled that the Pathé company would lease a permanent location in St. Augustine and continue making movies year-round; however, this hope did not materialize. On May 1 the motion picture troupe boarded a train to head homeward. A crowd gathered at the station to bid them farewell. One local woman, Maude Cook, accompanied Pathé property man Earl Woodland on the train as the new Mrs. Woodland.[26]

Another St. Augustinian who may have followed the Pathé crowd north was Willard Colee, a young man of twenty-three from a family with deep roots in Florida. Colee had played a bit part as an extra in *Pearl of the Punjab* alongside star Lillian Wiggins. Local man Joe Copps later told the story of a "handsome local boy of Spanish descent" who caught Wiggins' eye and whom she encouraged to come to New York. This story may or may not be true: Wiggins soon departed for Europe but Colee stayed in New York to make movies for Pathé and in later years for other companies. Colee would never rise to top billing on any movie, but he played supporting roles in a number of films throughout the 1920s. Whenever one of his screen appearances played in St. Augustine, the *Record* would invite local citizens to come and see one of their own who had actually made it in the movies. Eventually, Colee established a career for himself as a leading makeup artist in Hollywood.[27]

EDISON

In November 1913 the Edison company sent a large contingent of movie-makers to Florida. Some settled in Dixieland Park, a former amusement park on the south bank of the St. Johns River opposite downtown Jacksonville, but another group continued on to St. Augustine and made their headquarters in the Florida House. Directors A. Jay Williams and Richard Ridgely headed the group. Their intent was to exploit the old Spanish settings of the Ancient City to the maximum.[28]

Their first production, *A Night at the Inn,* is set at one of St. Augustine's most noted buildings, the old Vedder House on the bayfront standing next to Treasury Street, famous as the "Narrowest Street in America." (Edison's film was made just weeks before the 1914 fire destroyed the vintage building.) The ox and cart, already employed by Pathé in *Pearl of the Punjab,* appears to add an element of bygone days. Herbert Prior appears

Edison Company's *A Night at the Inn* used the Vedder House as the inn. The alley next to the building is Treasury Street, advertised as "The Narrowest Street in America." Herbert Prior, Mabel Trunnelle, and Bigelow Cooper (*left to right*) are the players. (From *Motography*)

Mabel Trunnelle contemplates an old diary in the garden of Dr. Andrew Anderson's home, Markland, the setting for *The Message of the Sun Dial*. (From *Kinetogram*)

as a traveler who is obliged to stop at a strange inn kept by Bigelow Cooper, who schemes to rob his guest. Cooper's daughter, Mabel Trunnelle, takes pity on the unfortunate sojourner, however, and saves his purse and perhaps his life.[29] Prior and Trunnelle had met and married when they were both actors on the live stage. They were among the first famous stage performers to venture into motion pictures, making films as early as 1907.

In their next film the Edison team used the home of Dr. Andrew Anderson, one of the town's leading citizens and a close friend of Henry Flagler (who had just died the previous summer). The Anderson home, Markland, which dated from before the Civil War, had recently been renovated to look like a classic Greek Revival mansion. Edison's *Kinetogram* magazine described it as a "beautiful old white house set among heavily shaded lawns." The story, *The Message of the Sun Dial*, is of two couples who experience parallel separations—one because of the Civil War and a modern couple who break up over a silly little quarrel. The girl, Mabel Trunnelle, discovers an old diary hidden under a sundial and decides that she will not be separated from her love as the earlier couple had been.[30] Most of Edison's other films were slight two-reelers; aside from *Romance of the Everglades,* set somewhere in Florida, they used St. Augustine to represent exotic locales like South America (*The Lovely Señorita*), Central America (*The Silent Death*), and Italy (*The Message in the Rose*).

The City Gate of St. Augustine provided the stage for a scene from *The Lovely Señorita*. Trunnelle is in the center. (From *Kinetogram*)

Elsie MacLeod and Yale Benner use the watchtower of Fort Marion as a vantage point in *The Silent Death*. (From *Kinetogram*)

The rustic bridge over the pool in the courtyard of the Hotel Alcazar has been a landmark in St. Augustine for more than a century, although a concrete bridge replaced the original in the early 1950s. Richard Tucker, Herbert Prior, and Mabel Trunnelle (*left to right*) stand in the foreground of a shot from *A Romance of the Everglades*. (From *Motography*)

Another Edison film, *Rorke's Drift* (1914), became a major production involving hundreds of people from the community, both as "supers" in the film and as spectators to the moviemaking action. The film is taken from an incident in the Anglo-Zulu War in South Africa when a band of African warriors overran a British outpost at a place called Rorke's Drift. This battle is portrayed again in two modern movies: *Zulu* (1964) and *Zulu Dawn* (1979).

For *Rorke's Drift* Edison needed two armies, and so recruited men from town. Joe Copps, many years later, recalled: "As early as 1913 us kids used to cut classes to work as extras, and I being a rather young British soldier in the movie *Rorke's Drift,* made along the white beach sand of St. Augustine's Anastasia Island."[31] Edison even took out an advertisement in the local newspaper inviting spectators to ride the electric trolley to the beach to watch the production.

The company brought down a stage crew from Jacksonville to build a hospital, trading post, and Zulu village. The Florida National Guard building, St. Francis Barracks, served in one scene as a British military headquarters. The Edison Company was quite proud of *Rorke's Drift,*

Local men and boys played Redcoats in *Rorke's Drift*. Townspeople and tourists turned out to watch filming of the drama. (Courtesy of St. Augustine Historical Society)

In *Rorke's Drift* residents of St. Augustine portraying English soldiers and Zulu war-riors fought it out on Anastasia Island, a stand-in for South Africa. Note that in the photo the sword blade and spear point have been removed, probably in the interests of safety until the cameras were ready to roll. (Courtesy of St. Augustine Historical Society)

declaring, "Our Florida players have spared no expense in producing this picture. A small army of white men and a great crowd of negroes were em-ployed. . . . The Florida scenery makes an ideal setting for Zulu Land and adds both beauty and realism to the film." Interestingly, the Zulus were played by black men from the area. In the noted D. W. Griffith movie *Birth of a Nation*, made the following year, black soldiers were largely portrayed by white men made up in blackface.[32] The *St. Augustine Record* estimated that 350–400 actors took part in the movie.[33]

ALL STAR FEATURE FILM CORPORATION

In January 1914, the St. Augustine Chamber of Commerce announced that another film company would be coming to town to make a motion picture version of the stage play *The Education of Mr. Pipp*, a comedy based on the popular drawings of Charles Dana Gibson. The "Gibson Girl" image had long served as the definition of the ideal woman of the late Victorian era: voluptuous, well dressed, elaborately coiffured, and imperiously above the admiration of mere men. The All Star Feature players registered at the modest St. George Hotel rather than the high-toned Hotel Ponce de Leon, the more natural habitat of a real Gibson Girl. Digby Bell, a well-known comedian from the stage, portrayed Mr. Pipp, while Kate Jepson was Mrs. Pipp, with Belle Daube and Edna Mae Wilson as their daughters. The movie was set in Pittsburg, New York, and France, with St. Augustine representing France. The lawn of Dr. Anderson's Markland residence served as the stage for some of the outdoor scenes.[34] After just a week in town, the All Star players concluded their "flying trip" and returned to New York.[35]

STELLAR FEATURE PHOTOPLAY COMPANY

A brand-new film company, Stellar, came to Florida in January to make its first motion picture. This film was based on an old-time live stage melodrama about the trials and tribulations of a professional gambler and his wife over a number of years. Edwin Forsberg played the lead, with Caroline French as his wife, in *Forgiven, or the Jack O'Diamonds*. Some of the scenes were filmed on a riverboat on the St. Johns River and others in Jacksonville. A reviewer noted, "So, also, are there many interesting bits of the oldest city in the United States. . . . The outdoor photography is of excellent quality."[36]

KALEM

The Kalem moviemakers dropped down from their newly constructed Jacksonville winter studio to take advantage of St. Augustine's antique architecture for a film revival of the old stage play *A Celebrated Case*. Mock

For *A Celebrated Case* Kalem erected a large outdoor stage to record the "indoors" of a palace. (Courtesy of George Eastman Museum)

From close up the illusion of being inside a great hall is almost perfect, except that the sharp shadows thrown on the floor from the strong sunlight reveal the outdoor set. Helen Lindroth, already an experienced stage actress, would continue making movies through the 1920s. (Courtesy of State Archives of Florida)

Some of the cast of *A Celebrated Case* rest next to the decorative fountain on the west lawn of the Hotel Ponce de Leon. Today the hotel has been turned into the central building of Flagler College and the fountain has been replaced by a swimming pool. (Courtesy of George Eastman Museum)

French soldiers muster on St. Francis Street in *A Celebrated Case*. The Tovar House (*left*) and the González-Alvarez House, known as the "Oldest House," stand in the background. (From *Motion Picture News*)

eighteenth-century French and English troops lined up on the marshes to blast away at each other with muskets, and Flagler's large Hotel Ponce de Leon functioned as a French château. *Motion Picture World* opined that St. Augustine made a good setting for the film: "The pictures were made in Florida, but the scenes are so well and artistically chosen that one is throughout reminded of La Belle France."[37] Alice Joyce and Guy Coombs played the leading roles, with Alice Hollister, who would enjoy top billing in later performances, as a supporting actress.

AETNA FILM COMPANY

In February a contingent of actors from the Aetna Film Company of New York took rooms at the Florida House and stayed in St. Augustine for nearly a month. They produced only one film, *The Zingara*, the tragic story of a gypsy queen (Christine Mayo) and an outsider (George Cowl) who fall in love. The gypsy camp is set amid live oaks, festooned with flowing Spanish moss, even though the setting is supposed to be Italy. The company's producer, Richard Sterling, declared that "St. Augustine is better

A cameraman records two well-dressed ladies strolling through the camp of the gypsies in *The Zingara*. (Courtesy of St. Augustine Historical Society)

than California for motion picture making. . . . We have been in Bermuda, Cuba, South America, and all over the United States, and I must say that St. Augustine's climate, scenery, and general environment are better than we have ever found at any other locality."[38] Sterling went on to say that Aetna would consider establishing a permanent studio in St. Augustine—but instead the company soon went out of business altogether.

The *Florida Times-Union* newspaper of neighboring Jacksonville took approving note of all the moviemaking activity in the Ancient City. "St. Augustine is gaining no end of notoriety and good advertising this season as an ideal location for the taking of moving pictures, and more of this class of work has been done here in the past few months than ever before in the long history of this famous resort." It appeared that motion picture making might become a permanent industry in St. Augustine.[39]

LUBIN

After having made movies in St. Augustine in the winter of 1913, the Lubin Company returned to its Florida Yacht Club home in Jacksonville for the 1913–1914 winter season. In March 1914 George Terwilliger, an old movie hand but a new director for Lubin, brought his wife and a company of players to St. Augustine and checked in to the Alcazar Hotel, where they found Pearl White and some of the Pathé people already ensconced.[40] Terwilliger had spent some years writing screenplays for other companies, but now Lubin hired him to direct.

Lubin purchased an old Herreshoff yacht, the *Cosette*, and to get their money's worth, made three movies that employed the yacht in their plotlines. In the first film, *The Debt*, Mary Keane is a showgirl who takes money from Earl Metcalfe and uses it to pay for an operation her mother needs. Metcalfe does not believe Keane's story of how she used the money, but she vows to repay him. Later Keane goes cruising on a yacht with an old friend of her father's, Herbert Fortier, but Fortier turns out to be a rake who tries to force himself on Keane. Metcalfe has followed the yacht in his own cruiser and rescues Keane from the deck of Fortier's vessel. In the end Keane and Metcalfe reconcile and agree to marry. The *Cosette* survives intact.[41]

In an unidentified movie, gypsies squabble in front of the old County Court House on Charlotte Street. The great fire of April 1914 destroyed the whole area. (Courtesy of St. Augustine Historical Society)

Lubin's cameramen record the death of the yacht *Cosette* for use in the films *The Man from the Sea* and *Three Men and a Woman*. (From *Motography*)

The yacht would not be so lucky in the next film, *Three Men and a Woman*. In this tale's climax—set off the coast of Panama but actually filmed in St. Augustine waters—the vessel catches fire and explodes. Earl Metcalfe tries to save Anna Luther by jumping overboard with her, and they cling to a piece of floating debris. Kempton Greene, who had attempted to kidnap Anna by tricking her into going on his yacht (also portrayed by the *Cosette*), has also survived and battles Metcalfe in the water before drowning.[42]

Lubin's publicity department released an interview with Greene that captured the ridiculous lengths to which movie companies went to publicize their films and actors. Greene said that he "had some unforgettable escapes" while in Florida. "I wouldn't mention them if they had been the usual exaggerations of the ordinary press agent, for an actor in pictures is expected to attach no importance to the daily risk of his life. But this was one degree more risky. A yacht was loaded with oil and set afire, the conflagration timed so it would end with the explosion of a chest of powder.

I was left aboard with orders to jump into the water at a certain moment. With the fire raging behind me and the powder due to explode within a minute I hesitated to plunge over the rail. Why? Because I saw three sharks swimming near the surface. I could either be blown to smithereens or be nibbled by the sea beasts. I plunged. By some miracle the sharks did not attack me."[43]

Lubin turned the burning of the yacht during the making of this scene into a spectacle for the entertainment of the people of St. Augustine. After the *Cosette* had been stripped of its engines and anything else of value, it was towed to a spot not far off the beach of Anastasia Island and anchored. Director Terwilliger invited spectators to take the trolley down to the beach to watch the fireworks. The vessel had been loaded with a cargo of coal tar, oakum, gasoline, kerosene, and "a nifty bunch of dynamite." Cloudy weather forced postponement of shooting for two days, but then, while the cameramen readied their equipment and spectators watched, the seaman in charge took a motorboat out and set a fire onboard—which produced a little smoke but no fire. This forced the intrepid seaman to venture out a second time, board the smoldering yacht, and start a second fire. This time the result was a nice plume of smoke, and, as the cameras whirred, an electrical impulse sent by underwater wire detonated the dynamite. This blew debris high into the air, but not far enough away to endanger the watchers on shore. Then the long-suffering *Cosette* settled bow-first beneath the waves.[44] Neither Kempton Greene nor any sharks were anywhere in sight.

Lubin employed the same action sequence in *The Man from the Sea*. In this film Kempton Greene and Earl Metcalfe play cards to determine which of them will wed Anna Luther. One man cheats, then locks his rival in the wireless room of a yacht and sets the vessel afire to sink it to the bottom of the ocean. The winner weds his prize, but then the couple begins to receive wireless messages from beneath the sea. Lubin constructed a water tank to create the illusion of a ghost sending messages from a watery grave. In the film's climax, Anna Luther drives a car off a pier to her death, and her guilty husband commits suicide. When *The Man from the Sea* debuted at the Orpheum, the local ad said, "See the actor plunge in North river from Usina's pier."[45]

In early May Terwilliger and the Lubin players departed St. Augustine for their home studio, having successfully taken film for three good motion pictures.[46]

VITAGRAPH

A few days before the Lubin crew left, a group of Vitagraph actors arrived and took rooms at the Buckingham Hotel, adjacent to Flagler's Alcazar and Ponce de Leon hotels.[47] Newly widowed Sidney Drew headed the team as director and lead actor. Drew and his recently deceased wife, Gladys, had long been famous as a comedy team on the vaudeville circuit and in early one-reel comedies. He had good theater blood, being uncle to Lionel, John, and Ethel Barrymore. The female lead who played opposite him was Edith Storey, a prolific actress who had starred mostly in Westerns because of her proficiency at riding horses. Lucille McVey, who used the stage name Jane Morrow, played another leading female role.

In *A Florida Enchantment* the city St. Augustine got to play itself, not some faraway, fictitious locale. The film was based on a novel by Archibald Clavering Gunter, who had stayed at the Hotel Ponce de Leon years earlier. Sidney Drew was cast as the house physician of the Ponce de Leon, and many scenes take place on the grounds of the hotel. The hotel's custodian, James McGuire, wrote company headquarters in New York, requesting permission for Vitagraph to shoot inside the hotel, but evidently the answer was no since all the interior scenes were made before a nondescript stage backdrop. The home of Storey's uncle is the Knight house on Oneida Street, which had recently been used in *Pearl of the Punjab* and *Perils of Pauline*. Other venues that appear in the story are Fort Marion, St. George Street, Dr. Garnett's orange grove, and the municipal pier.[48]

A Florida Enchantment is perhaps the best known of the silent films produced in Florida, partly because it has survived while the vast majority of other nitrate cellulose films made at the time have turned to vinegar vapor and dust. It may have unappreciated historical significance as the first full-length comedy produced, since it precedes the better-known Mack Sennett/Charlie Chaplin comedy *Tillie's Punctured Romance* by several months.

Cast members of *A Florida Enchantment* pose in the courtyard of the Hotel Ponce de Leon. Edith Storey wears men's clothing and a mustache after her extraordinary transformation. Storey smiles at actress Lucille McVey, who would marry the film's star, Sidney Drew, shortly after making this movie. (From *Motography*)

The film has also gained notoriety in recent years because it deals with gender identity. In the film Storey discovers mysterious African seeds secreted in an old sea captain's chest she purchases at Dodge's Old Curiosity Shop (today's Parades-Dodge House) on St. George Street. The strange seeds possess the power to change the sex of anyone who consumes them.

The controversial part of the film, even when the film was first exhibited, comes when Storey sees Drew treating the "sprained wrist" of a designing woman, played by Ada Gifford, and driven by jealousy, decides to swallow a seed, become a man, and behave in the loutish way that men do. After being transformed, but still dressed as a woman, she embraces and kisses several women—the notorious part of the film. Later, when Storey discloses her secret to Drew, he refuses to believe her and she challenges him to try a seed himself. After gulping down the seed, Drew immediately assumes comedic feminine mannerisms. Later the now-female Drew, dressed in women's clothing, is chased around the city by police and a mob of pursuers until, in desperation, he/she leaps off the end of the municipal pier and sinks beneath the waves. At this point Storey awakens; her real-life fiancé, Drew, enters the room; and Storey realizes it has all been a dream.

In modern times some scholars have embraced the film as an early gay-lesbian–themed feature. This interpretation hinges on whether the magic of the seeds leads to an actual biological transformation of the characters or simply an alteration of sexual orientation. Evidently, this possibility of nuanced interpretations of the film's sexual content was evident to contemporary reviewers and caused them some discomfort over the movie's possibly implicit messages. Race also becomes mixed with gender in some modern reviewers' interpretations, since Storey's black maid, played by Ethel Lloyd, is forced to swallow a seed too in order to be transformed into a valet. Lloyd and other white actors don blackface to portray the "colored" characters in the film and behave according to the standard racist norms of blackface comedy. The fact that Lloyd is obviously a white woman eases the racial/sexual tension that would be created by having an actual black woman become a man and mingle in a household of white women.[49]

Vitagraph's founder and president, J. Stuart Blackton, was in town during the making of the movie to attend the Southern Power Boat Championships, which were being contested on Matanzas Bay. His boat, the *Hydro-Bullet*, ranked as one of the fastest in the races. Blackton gave the *Hydro-Bullet* a part in one brief scene of *A Florida Enchantment*. While Drew and Gifford are rowing a skiff out to an anchored yacht, the speedboat appears out of nowhere and recklessly sideswipes Drew's rowboat, dumping the two actors into the bay.[50]

Local boy Joe Copps later remembered Blackton's stay at the Hotel Ponce de Leon. He described the "Commodore" as "quite a gay fellow" who was arrested along with some friends in the dark hours of one early morning trying to climb up an old balcony, and consequently spent the rest of the night in jail.[51]

The Vitagraph company departed St. Augustine in mid-May, saying that they hoped to return again someday. (It would be 1920 before they came back.) The *St. Augustine Record* estimated that they had brought $7,000 into the local economy during their stay.[52]

The Moving Picture Girls Under the Palms

Laura Lee Hope

The Moving Picture Girls Under the Palms follows a group of fictional teenagers who make movies in St. Augustine and in the wilds of Florida. (Courtesy of St. Augustine Historical Society)

A Florida Enchantment worked its magic on Sidney Drew. A few weeks after his return north he married Lucille McVey, a cast member, and together they would form another "Mr. and Mrs. Sidney Drew" comedy team.

St. Augustine figured into the moviemaking world in another way in 1914. Grosset & Dunlap, publishers of the popular Bobbsey Twins books for young readers, brought out the fourth installment of its Moving Picture Girls series, entitled *Under the Palms, or Lost in the Wilds of Florida*.

These books, aimed at early-teen girls, involved a gang of teen actresses who traveled around the country making movies and encountering adventures along the way. In this book the girls arrive in St. Augustine to shoot scenes for "The Spanish Prisoner." They stay in a large hotel having an inner courtyard with a spraying fountain—evidently either the Ponce de Leon or the Alcazar. The producer, it was explained, "had not spared expense in taking out his moving picture company. And he had a method in going to one of the largest and finest hotels in St. Augustine. He intended to stage some scenes of one of the Southern plays there, and having his actors and actresses right in the hotel made it more practical."[53]

The Moving Picture Girls visit the major attractions in St. Augustine: Fort Marion, the Fountain of Youth (where they sample the water), Garnett's orange grove, the Alligator Farm, the Slave Market, and the City Gates. The powerboat races make for an exciting element in the story, as one of the girls risks her neck and a boat capsizes. From St. Augustine— "The most gorgeous place I ever saw," says one girl—they venture into the alligator-infested interior of Florida for more danger, mystery, and adventure.[54]

With the arrival of summer in Florida, the filmmaking season came to an end. It had been quite a prolific few months for St. Augustine. Nine different companies had spent time in town, and they accumulated reels of film for twenty-two motion pictures. Most of these were five-reel "feature films," not the one-reel shorts from just a couple of years earlier. The Chamber of Commerce could take pride in the results of its efforts to lure moviemakers to the city, and the future looked bright for even greater success in the coming year.

4

A FOOL THERE WAS

1915

A Fool there was and he made his prayer
To a rag and a bone and a hank of hair
We called her the woman who did not care
But the fool he called her his lady fair.

Rudyard Kipling

FOX FILM CORPORATION

The enterprise that became a major studio all started without much notice. In November 1914, the *St. Augustine Record* ran a brief story that a
small New York film production company called Box Office Attractions
had been working on a movie in St. Augustine and were headquartered at
the Monson Hotel on the bayfront. The company had gone over to Jacksonville for a few days but would soon return. Cloudy weather had slowed
their progress, although they expected to finish their work and sail for
New York soon. The movie in production was entitled *A Fool There Was*,
and William Fox, with his new company Fox Film Corporation, would
soon replace Box Office Attractions.[1]

The film was completed in a hurry and premiered on January 12, 1915,
at one of William Fox's theaters, The Strand in New York City. An an-
nouncer read Kipling's poem as the Strand orchestra played the movie
theme music to "a ghastly blue glare from the footlights." Then the six

reels of *A Fool There Was* followed. The reviewer for *Moving Picture World* condemned the film as "a production which, but for the interpolation of a few beautiful and realistic bits of home life, reeks with the foulness, the sorrow, and the horrible consequences of the life wasted in the toils of a human vampire. . . . Sin has been presented in its most revolting aspects."[2]

Fox took out a full-page ad in *Motion Picture News* declaring his movie to be "the greatest photoplay production in history. . . . $100,000 worth of women's gowns shown. . . . Wonderful sets arranged with Tiffany, New York. . . . Gorgeous Florida Outdoor Scenery—The Fountain of Youth."[3]

Fox hired two reporters from the *New York World* to stage a publicity appearance of the film's then-unknown leading woman, Theda Bara, at Chicago's Blackstone Hotel. Bara, draped in furs, made an appearance but pretended to be unable to speak English. As reporters scribbled notes, Fox's publicity men explained that she had come to America from Paris to escape the outbreak of World War I. Her parents, Giuseppe Bara, a French sculptor, and her mother, Theda de Lyre, a French actress, had met in Egypt and lived in a tent near the Sphinx. Theda Bara had been acting on the stage in Paris before coming to America. The reporters were intrigued by this story even though they felt pretty sure they were being put on. The mystery of Bara's origins added to the publicity value of the Blackstone Hotel introduction. Later someone noticed that the letters of her name could be rearranged to spell "Arab Death."

In actuality Theodosia Goodman was a Jewish girl from Cincinnati who had been acting on the stage in the United States for years in minor parts and had made her film debut as an extra in Pathé's *The Stain* in 1914. Bara's appearance in *A Fool There Was* transformed her overnight into a screen sensation and made William Fox a major player in the film industry. For a few years Bara would keep up the pretense of the Egyptian-origin story, but eventually everyone accepted it for the publicity sham that it was.

When the movie was released, some publicity pieces gave top billing to Edward José, the "Fool." A dignified older actor who really had been born abroad (in Brussels), José had already enjoyed years of experience in live theater as a pianist, actor, and director. The previous year he had appeared in *Perils of Pauline*. He began his movie career with Pathé before moving

Edward José appears to be helplessly in the clutches of Theda Bara in this publicity still for *A Fool There Was*. (Courtesy of MoviestillsDB)

over to Fox. Clifford Bruce made the same transition, playing the role of best friend to José in *A Fool There Was*.

In the film Bara, the femme fatale, selects José, a wealthy businessman, as her next prey. Early in the story one of Bara's earlier victims pleads with her to take him back and even points a revolver at her. She responds with, "Kiss me, my fool," and he turns the gun on himself, committing suicide. Bara proceeds to place herself in the path of José, who is traveling by steamer to Europe as a U.S. diplomat. He has been obliged to leave his wife and daughter behind to tend to the wife's injured sister.

Not many scenes later we find José reclining on the breast of Bara in Italy—probably actually in the backyard of the Knight house on Oneida Street, as several of the episodes seem to be set at this house. The court-yard of the Hotel Alcazar serves, appropriately, as the entrance to a hotel, and later José's wife enters Flagler's Grace Methodist Church to pray for her husband. Many of the other scenes take place in Jacksonville and, apparently, in New York City.

Except for one negligee scene, Bara is always dressed in luxurious gowns to emphasize the temptations of extravagance. No sex, not even passionate kissing, is depicted on screen, and Bara's sexual hold over José is suggested only by his slow degeneration into a pathetic addict. The movie established Bara as Fox's biggest attraction and made her an emblematic figure in American popular culture: The Vamp.

ALL STAR FEATURE FILMS

Another film company worked in St. Augustine in November of 1914 at the same time as Box Office. The All Star players, who had produced *The Education of Mr. Pipp* the previous winter season, came back to make another motion picture. They returned to their former quarters in the St. George Hotel and again shot some of their scenes on the lawn of Dr. Anderson's Markland estate. Two noted actors, William Russell (formerly in town with Thanhouser) and Jane Cowl, headed the cast. After just ten days the company packed their bags and returned to Fort Lee, New Jersey, to finish the indoor scenes.[4]

Their film, *The Garden of Lies,* is built around the sort of convoluted love triangle that was stock-in-trade for movies of that era. Jane Cowl plays an American girl who has married a foreign prince, portrayed by Philip Hahn. On the very day of their wedding Cowl is injured in a fall from a carriage and loses her memory. Shortly thereafter her new husband is called away to claim the throne of his small European kingdom. Cowl's health deteriorates, and her physicians determine that only the return of her husband can save her. Enter William Russell, who had admired Cowl from afar as she walked in the garden of her home. Cowl initially believes that Russell is her husband, returned from abroad, but soon her real husband returns. Hahn and Russell duel with swords for the right to continue as Cowl's husband. Cowl's memory returns just as kidnappers from Hahn's kingdom abduct her. Both Hahn and Russell rush to her rescue. Hahn is killed and Russell is gravely wounded. Only Cowl's love can save him from dying in despair.[5]

Cowl seems to have enjoyed making the film. She gave an interview, perhaps with tongue in cheek, to an entertainment magazine about the film's swordfight: "As I saw the duel fought in St. Augustine it was no slight affair. William Russell, the pretended husband, and Philip Hahn, who played the prince husband, were somewhat cut and slashed after it was over."[6]

PEERLESS PICTURES

Peerless Pictures Producing Company of Fort Lee, New Jersey, enjoyed only a brief life before being absorbed into World Film Corporation in May of 1915. In January 1915, however, it had two of the brightest stars in moviedom working in St. Augustine: Howard Estabrook and Barbara Tennant (heroine of the previous year's *Sons of a Soldier*). Oscar A. C. Lund was producer and director. Their movie, *The Butterfly*, opens in Egypt and moves to Europe then America. Flagler's Hotels Alcazar and Ponce de Leon serve as locations for some scenes. Tennant is the Butterfly, a famous dancer, who is accused of murder, and Estabrook is one of her lovers who finally rescues her from both the police and the real murderer.[7]

The film crew of an unidentified movie shoot a scene on the front portico of the Hotel Ponce de Leon. Note the reflector held by a technician to focus sunlight on the actors. (Courtesy of State Archives of Florida)

The cast of *M'Liss* poses for a group photo. Barbara Tennant (*center*) appears intimidated by the crowd, which includes director Oscar A. C. Lund (*extreme right*) who plays the malevolent Don Jose in the movie. (Courtesy of St. Augustine Historical Society)

The second film made by the Peerless troupe was a movie rendition of the Bret Harte novel *M'Liss*, which had enjoyed a long run on the live stage. Interestingly, in this motion picture Florida is used as a stand-in for California, and North Carolina furnishes mountains that are supposed to be in Nevada. Barbara Tennant plays Melissa Smith, a spunky western girl whose father dies and leaves her a fortune in oil-rich property—except that her father's will is found by Don Jose, played by Oscar A. C. Lund, who conceals the will and establishes himself as M'Liss's guardian.

The oilfield is in California, and the conclusion of the film takes place there. Howard Estabrook is a schoolmaster who had loved M'Liss in Nevada and follows her to California, where he discovers oil next to M'Liss's property. At the conclusion Lund and Estabrook engage in a fistfight as the oilfields burn. Lund perishes, leaving Estabrook and Tennant to live happily ever after.[8]

J. E. Brulatour, the president of Peerless, dropped in on his crew in St. Augustine. During an interview with the *St. Augustine Record* he compared Florida favorably with California, noting that Florida was only thirty-two hours away from New York whereas the train ride to California took five days. He noted the obvious, that Florida lacked the grand mountains of the West, but he added that St. Augustine did have tropical vegetation, Spanish-style buildings, and the old fort.[9]

Brulatour had another crew at work in Jacksonville on a movie version of the stage play *What Happened to Jones*. Fred Mace both directed and starred in this comedy. The movie skipped from one comic encounter to another and involved a variety of settings, some located in St. Augustine.[10]

DYREDA ART FILM CORPORATION

In March Howard Estabrook returned to St. Augustine as the lead actor in *Four Feathers*, a film produced by the Dyreda Art Film Corporation. This 1915 silent film was based on the 1902 novel by English writer A.E.W. Mason and, as it turned out, would be just the first of three motion picture versions of the novel made over the years. The title comes from the custom of handing a white feather to a coward who fails to do his duty in battle. In this case Estabrook receives three white feathers from his soldier-compatriots in Britain's war in the Sudan. The fourth feather comes from his sweetheart, Irene Warfield. To redeem himself Estabrook disguises himself as an Arab musician and travels into the desert to free his captive comrades. St. Augustine and the sand dunes of Anastasia Island stand in for the Sudan, although some scenes were made at Atlantic Beach east of Jacksonville and interiors were filmed in New York City.[11]

The filming on the streets of St. Augustine led to one humorous episode involving Estabrook. As recounted in the *St. Augustine Record*: "Yesterday he was all ready in the automobile on Granada Street, 'made up like

Howard Estabrook, disguised as a native, drags one of his comrades to safety in the deserts of the Sudan—located somewhere on Anastasia Island. (From the author's collection)

the chap in the Mogul cigarette box but without the whiskers,' as he put it, when the cloudy weather cancelled the motion picture work for the day." So he walked down Granada to the Oriental bazaar shop, stepped behind the counter, and waited on customers, speaking broken English. He sold some handkerchiefs and beads and was trying to sell a rug when someone gave the joke away.[12] The "Oriental shop" was a rug emporium operated by the Mussallem family, who had recently purchased the exotic Villa Zorayda and the Granada Hotel next door (which they renamed the Alhambra Hotel). Today the Mussallem family still owns the Zorayda and opens it as a house museum.

Dyreda had a second team of actors and technicians at work on *Always in the Way*, which had already taken some tropical scenes in Bermuda and took some more in St. Augustine. A portion of the film is set in Africa, with Mary Miles Minter as the adopted daughter of missionaries. Minter, who was only thirteen years old at the time, had been on the stage since the age of five. She won fame in the play *The Littlest Rebel*. Her mother, Charlotte Shelby, always traveled with Mary and even played a minor role in this movie. Minter's sweet face and golden ringlets soon made her one of the silent screen's most popular and recognizable stars.

Dyreda even had a third unit of actors at work on what was described as a multi-reel comedy with Franklin Coates as a jungle explorer and Laura Sawyer as his love interest. This film used animals from the Johnny Jones one-ring circus, which happened to be in town. Among them was a large, old tiger named King who was taken to a fenced-in area outside of town in order to shoot a scene. At first the tiger enjoyed napping, but he took exception to his trainers' efforts to maneuver him into position for the actors and cameraman. Eventually, the scene was successfully completed.[13]

The fate of this comedy is a mystery. A May 1915 story in *Variety* magazine said that the Dyreda comedy, "not titled as yet," was in final stages of production, but evidently it was never released. The greater mystery is what happened to the film's star, Laura Sawyer. She had been a prominent performer for Edison and then for Famous Players, but this Dyreda production was evidently the last film she ever worked on. Her contract with Dyreda ended that spring, and she disappeared from the film world, except for being credited with the script for the 1917 Famous Players' movie *The Valentine Girl*. After that, so far as we know, she lived quietly and raised a family in the New York area, before passing away in 1970.[14]

FAMOUS PLAYERS

In the winter of 1915 Sidney Olcott returned to St. Augustine as director for a new company, Famous Players. Noted for his direction of the 1907 epic *Ben Hur*, Olcott had earlier directed *The Seminole's Vengeance* (1908) and *In Old Florida* (1911) in St. Augustine for Kalem. Although Olcott had been elevated to the presidency of Kalem, his salary remained so low that he accepted Mary Pickford's invitation to join Famous Players Film Company. His new motion picture *The Moth and the Flame* was based on a story that had played on the live stage many times before. Olcott used Flagler's hotels as settings for the story of a woman, played by Adele Ray,

THE COURTING OF A ROMANCE

DANIEL FROHMAN
PRESENTS
THE MOTH AND THE FLAME
PRODUCED BY
FAMOUS PLAYERS
BY LASKY CORPORATION

The Moth and the Flame used Flagler's hotels for the setting of a story of love, deceit, and redemption. Here Adele Ray and Bradley Barker meet next to the rustic bridge in the courtyard of the Hotel Alcazar. (Courtesy of Silent Film Still Archive)

who is so blinded by love she cannot see that the man she is prepared to marry is a cad. At the wedding ceremony a woman stands up in the audience—melodramatically holding the illegitimate child of the groom. With the blinding light of a nearly fatal attraction removed, Adele's character finds a new love, played by Bradley Barker. Neatly bringing the tale to conclusion, the would-be groom decides to take back the woman and child he had wronged.[15]

January 1915 found George Terwilliger and his "nomad" band of Lubin moviemakers back in St. Augustine, in the familiar confines of the Hotel Alcazar. His leading players from the previous year, Ormi Hawley, Mary Keane, Earl Metcalfe, Kempton Greene, and Herbert Fortier were among the crew. Lubin announced that they would move on to other locations in Florida then travel to Cuba for tropical scenery. However, they ultimately decided to remain in St. Augustine, for, as the *St. Augustine Record* explained: "St. Augustine offers all advantages. City scenes have been taken here, South African and Arabian on the dunes and sands of the ocean beach, marine scenes, Spanish scenes—almost any kind of story may be filmed here to advantage, the ancient and the modern St. Augustine offering a variety of settings to be found no where else. This fact is being recognized more and more by the moving picture people and is adding much to the fame of the Ancient City."[16]

Adele Ray and Bradley Barker stand in the carriage path behind the Hotel Ponce de Leon. The balcony and Tiffany windows of the hotel's dining room can be seen in the background. (Courtesy of Silent Film Still Archive)

Terwilliger wrote, directed, and produced all the films made in St. Augustine that winter. They were easy-to-produce two- and three-reelers that depended upon action for their appeal. The first made, *The Hermit of Bird Island*, took its name from an actual sandbar at the mouth of St. Augustine's inlet. The story used film footage shot the previous year in the powerboat championship races. Kempton Greene appears as a haughty English earl who owns a powerful racing boat, but injury prevents him from piloting it. His fiancée, Mary Keane, induces a local fisherman, Earl Metcalfe, to race the earl's vessel. During the race Mary flies overhead in an airplane shouting encouragement to Metcalfe. (The airplane was actually George Gray's Wright Flyer that had appeared in the previous year's *Perils of Pauline*.) Metcalfe wins the race but discovers that Keane is betrothed to the earl. Disappointed, he swims out to sea, intending to end it all. Instead he washes up on a deserted island. Meanwhile Greene seduces Keane's cousin, Hazel Hubbard, and a horrified Keane paddles a canoe out to sea, drifting up on the same island inhabited by Metcalfe. Metcalfe builds a hut for Keane and secretly brings her food, but stays out of sight. Ultimately, Greene stops by the island to explore, finds Keane, makes improper advances, and is beaten by Metcalfe in a fistfight. Keane and Metcalfe decide to marry and live on the island. Once again, as in the previous year's *Three Men and a Woman*, Greene gets beaten up by Metcalfe and loses the girl.[17]

The girl shown in the scene of the canoe paddling away into the ocean was not actress Mary Keane but local girl Kathryn Oliveros, who happened to have blonde hair. She later recounted how two movie men knocked on her front door and asked her to stand in for Keane. She had never paddled a canoe and did not know how to swim, but she took the assignment because, as she said, she "liked a lark." Her husband, Gard, accompanied her to Corbett's Dock and gave her a quick lesson in how to paddle a canoe. While a director shouted at her through a megaphone and an assistant reflected sunshine onto her golden locks with a large mirror, she performed the sequence eight times.[18]

In early March Terwilliger invited some of the local townsfolk to the Alcazar Casino to watch a preview screening of *The Hermit of Bird Island*. The Lubin crew and the St. Augustine people enjoyed seeing familiar homes and gardens, the water near the lighthouse, and the entrance to

Fort Marion, but no one from town recognized Kathryn Oliveros making her movie debut.[19]

Oliveros would later recall that the casino's huge indoor swimming pool was used in a scene for some picture in which the balcony surrounding the pool stood in for the deck of an ocean liner, and a local man was filmed falling off the "deck" and into the "ocean" below.[20]

Terwilliger's next creation exploited more sequences from the powerboat races. *The Cipher Key* has South American secret agents Herbert Fortier and Kempton Greene chasing shipbuilder Earl Metcalfe and his girlfriend, Mary Keane, all over the east coast of Florida, seeking a secret code U.S. Navy battleships used for communication. This plot is an excuse for an airplane to chase an automobile until both vehicles wreck; then the pursuit continues in racing boats until the unfortunate Greene once more bites the dust—or, rather, surf.[21]

W. Livingston Larned, a winter visitor who penned occasional columns of ruminations for the *St. Augustine Record*, enjoyed watching the movie men and women at their craft. He wrote in one issue,

> At the old Spanish fort, down the quiet, sleepy, drowsy streets; on the wide white immaculate beach as the green tide rolls restlessly in; along palm shaded avenues; through the beautiful gardens of the Ponce and Alcazar; before a quaint little curio shop, hundreds of years old; on the slopes of the fort green, with the Matanzas flowing drowsily in the distance, or beneath the great striped lighthouse on Anastasia Island—everywhere you will find them—these industrious movie folks. Children of toil and sunshine, bless their busy hearts.[22]

On one occasion Larned informed his readers of a conversation he recently overheard: "Movie Actor—'Mr. X. what are we to do this morning?' Movie Director—'Well, this a.m. I want to shoot you at the fort, stab you in the Arsenal and finally blow you up with a mine just off Corbett's oyster dock. It's sort of a quiet day. I'm not feeling myself.'"[23]

Another day's column brought readers a vignette from the life of Lubin's director: "Terwilliger had a way of getting up in the morning, yawning, stretching, and saying, 'Let's see, little company. None of that ordinary cheap junk today. I feel as if some snake scenes would set well. Harry, run out and get me a boa constrictor.'" The Johnny Jones Circus,

Ormi Hawley was known more for her spunky personality than for good looks. She appeared in dozens of silent films. (From *Motion Picture Magazine*)

also exploited by Dyreda, happened to have "a big reptile on file" named "Lucy."[24]

The only motion picture made by Lubin in St. Augustine in 1915 that features a snake was apparently *The Man of God*. (Since this ephemeral two-reel drama has not survived, its exact contents are today unknown.) The story involves two survivors of a shipwreck, Ormi Hawley and Kempton Greene, who wash up on an island inhabited by a religious hermit, Earl Metcalfe. At first Metcalfe welcomes the castaways and invites them all to live in peace, but Greene turns out to be an "evil man." Predictably, Metcalfe and Greene end up in a fistfight, but it is a poisonous snake that does the unfortunate Greene in this time. A rescue party takes Hawley away, leaving Metcalfe in his solitude as before.[25]

The "burned over district" from St. Augustine's 1914 fire still remained a desolate scene of destruction after the passage of a year. Remnants of some smoke-blackened stone walls stood as monuments to the conflagration. Terwilliger decided to use a portion of these ruins for a film, *The Insurrection*, that involved the destruction of a South American coastal town. The old Spanish chimney and well on the Beach Road, which had previously figured in *Pearl of the Punjab*, makes another appearance. Then Terwilliger also found some abandoned buildings on Anastasia Island that could be fixed up as simple village dwellings—suitable for destruction in the climax of his movie.[26]

In *The Insurrection* Earle Metcalfe plays the role of a U.S. Navy lieutenant who loves Ormi Hawley, daughter of a South American revolutionary. Her father, Herbert Fortier, captures Metcalfe and locks him in a prison; he then confines Hawley in her bedroom to prevent her from warning U.S. Navy warships standing offshore of an impending rebellion. Fortunately, Metcalfe has taught his lover the signal code used by the Navy, and she waves a handkerchief out her window to warn the Navy men. (This is a movie, after all!) Battleships—evidently taken from stock film of Navy exercises—blast away at the town, destroying it in explosions and fire. Fortunately, both Metcalfe and Ormi escape unscathed and flee the rebels to join the American forces at sea.[27]

Terwilliger and his intrepid trio of Hawley, Metcalfe, and Greene (joined sometimes by Hazel Hubbard) completed three other short dramas: *Destiny's Skein*, *The Last Rebel*, and *The Telegrapher's Peril*, before returning north at the end of March. Altogether they had produced seven motion pictures during their stay in town. Lubin ended up being the most prolific moviemaking company during St. Augustine's brief history as a film center. Since the first film in 1910, Lubin had made thirteen films in town.

Reflecting on his experiences, George Terwilliger said, "It's no joke to be sent away for a few months at a time and be told to send in pictures. You write them as you go along, manage your company, get your locations, and do all your business besides directing."[28]

Terwilliger would leave Lubin in early 1916, and perhaps this was a sign of Lubin's impending demise. Unfortunately, Lubin Manufacturing Company, one of the earliest filmmakers, had not adapted to changing times in the movie industry. While more successful companies had turned to producing higher-quality five-reel feature films, Lubin continued churning out two- and three-reel shorts of modest quality. The outbreak of World War I curtailed Lubin's profitable European market. Efforts to merge with stronger firms proved unsuccessful, and on September 1, 1916, Lubin went out of business.

KALEM

St. Augustine's old friends from the Kalem Company dropped down early in 1915 from their new studio in Jacksonville to shoot a few scenes for *The White Goddess*. Alice Joyce, who had played the lead in *A Celebrated Case*, appears as an English woman who is worshiped as a goddess by Hindus when she travels to India. The interior scenes were made in the Jacksonville studio, but some "Oriental" exteriors were shot at Fort Marion and perhaps at other St. Augustine locales.[29]

The Kalem players paid another brief visit in May to shoot some scenes for the old stage play set in Spain, *Don Caesar de Bazan*. They wanted to carry off a swordfight on the fort's terreplein, exploit the ruins from the fire, and use some old and new Spanish-style residences as settings. Italian-born director Robert G. Vignola directed the film. The experienced English stage actor W. Lawton Butt played the headline role of Don Caesar, with Alice Hollister (*A Celebrated Case*) as the female lead. *Moving Picture World* put its stamp of approval on the result, declaring, "The

Alice Hollister can claim to be the first "vamp," since she appeared in that role in Kalem's *The Vampire* (1913). Here she looks pretty harmless standing at one of the ladies' entrances to the Hotel Ponce de Leon. (From *Motion Picture Magazine*)

Alice Hollister and the cast of *Don Caesar de Bazan* pose in the courtyard of the Hotel Ponce de Leon. (Courtesy of State Archives of Florida)

backgrounds, chosen in old St. Augustine, with care so that one never sees discordant notes or jarring incongruities, serve almost, if not quite as well as old Madrid would have served—the scenes are perfect even if they don't contain the Escorial."[30]

OCEAN FILM COMPANY

Sometime probably in the late winter or early spring of 1915 film producers from a newly formed company paid a brief three-day visit to St. Augustine to take some scenes. Ocean Film Company had just been organized by a group of anonymous men headquartered in New York. Jesse J. Goldburg, well known in movie circles, served as general manager and wrote the screenplay for the company's first production, *Life Without Soul*—an adaptation of Mary Shelley's *Frankenstein*. It would be the first full-length Frankenstein motion picture made, although Edison had released a twelve-minute short in 1910.[31]

The movie crew traveled from New York to Jacksonville to St. Augustine to Dahlonega, Georgia, and back to New York, taking scenes for the film. Thanks to all this travel the movie received acclaim for the epic sweep of its cinematography. In the story a young physician, Victor Frawley, played by William Cohill, concocts a fluid with the remarkable ability to impart life to inanimate objects. While pondering the implications of his discovery, he begins reading Shelley's book. Dr. Frawley, like Dr. Frankenstein, dares to create a man, called in the film "The Creation." Percy Standing, an experienced vaudeville actor new to the movies, plays the creature. He is not transformed into a monster by heavy makeup, but relies on his own imposing physical presence to appear as more than a natural man. The reviewer for *Motography* magazine wrote, "The superman, a creature of superb physique who, without conscience, makes no attempt to restrain the cravings of his healthy body, is an exceptionally suspenseful figure for the photoplay. Neither all man nor all beast, his actions can be fashioned to suit the requirements of a dramatic situation and still be in keeping with that which the spectator expects of a creature so strange."[32]

William Cohill, Lucy Cotton, and Percy Standing (*left to right*) played the leading roles in *Life Without Soul*. (From *Moving Picture World*)

The audience finds The Creation a sympathetic figure, at least at first, for he comes to realize that he is alone in the world. In his anguish he begins killing those who love Dr. Frawley—his little sister, his friend, and finally the doctor's bride as well. Frawley realizes that he must destroy the monster he has made and pursues him from place to place. In one scene the monster throws the entire crew of a sailing ship overboard. Finally, Dr. Frawley traps The Creation in a mine and dynamites the entrance to seal the monster inside, but this exertion takes the doctor's last scrap of energy, and he dies. At that point Dr. Frawley awakens from his dream with Shelley's book in his lap.[33]

The movie created a sensation when released. Some theater owners judged the film "in advance of the time," and the board of censors in the state of Pennsylvania banned showing of the movie. Nevertheless, demand for the movie was so great that the film was re-edited to add some "scientific" footage about cell division and blood circulation. Color "tinting and toning" was added to some scenes to create a more dramatic atmosphere.[34] Unfortunately, no surviving copies of this intriguing film have been found.

FOX

In May 1915, after the close of the tourist season, Fox's Frank Powell, who had directed A Fool There Was, brought Theda Bara and a cast of actors and technicians to St. Augustine for filming of The Devil's Daughter. Clifford Bruce once again had a part to play in the drama. The company returned to the Monson Hotel and spilled over into the equally modest Marion Hotel. It was unusual for film crews to appear in Florida in the summertime, and Fox's press releases stressed the hot weather that drove the New Yorkers to visit the beach for a swim. Bara, by now famous as the "vamp," was described as wearing "an Italian one-piece bathing garment of flaming scarlet." Of course, the press release also stressed the dangers from "moccasin snakes," toe-pinching crabs in the surf, and ominous shark fins gliding by in deeper water.[35] Powell and his players left near the end of May, having spent just two weeks filming scenes, but Powell said that he would return later in the fall for a much more elaborate production.[36]

Producer Frank Powell sits amidst the actors and crew of *The Devil's Daughter* on St. Augustine Beach. Child actress Jane Lee sits at his feet, and Theda Bara is on his right. (From the author's collection)

The Devil's Daughter is set in Florence, and several local buildings were employed for their Italianate look. The Villa Flora, a private home of yellow brick and coquina stone, which was noted for its rose garden, played a prominent role, as did the Hotel Ponce de Leon and Hotel Alcazar. Dr. Garnett's orange grove north of town also appeared in some scenes. The story is the sordid tale of a young woman who is deserted by her lover and thereafter vows eternal vengeance against all men.

Motion Picture News anticipated that the movie would show off Bara to her great advantage: "This remarkable young woman, who possesses a type of beauty which is described by artists and sculptors to be of absolute unique character, has become a literally international figure since first she burst upon us from Le Theatre Antoine, Paris, in the William Fox production of *A Fool There Was*. . . . Many newspapers throughout the country declared her to be the most wickedly beautiful actress in the world."[37] The magazine's reviewer apparently was still buying the line that Bara had grown up in the Middle East and Europe.

Moving Picture World's reviewer took a jaundiced view of the whole movie. *The Devil's Daughter* "seems like a rather poor imitation of *A Fool There Was*. . . . Being all in a lugubrious key, the picture becomes wearisome and occasionally—when comedy was the farthest from the intention of the actors—laughable." However, the critic found the Florida settings attractive.[38]

The 1914–1915 cool-weather season had been an excellent one for St. Augustine as a movie production location. The town could lay claim to seventeen locally made motion pictures, and some of them were quite good. Florida seemed to be holding its own against Southern California as a place to make movies, although one by one eastern companies were building substantial studios in the Los Angeles area. For example, Universal City was being developed near Los Angeles as a complex erected from the ground up solely for the purpose of making movies. The other dark cloud on the horizon was the outbreak of the Great War in Europe, and no one could predict how badly that might impact the international exchange of motion pictures.

5

EGYPT ON THE GULF STREAM

1915–1916

At mid-decade St. Augustine entered into its most productive years as a movie-making center; yet changes in the cinema industry—both nationally and in Florida—would soon send the film producers away from the Old City. For the moment, however, things seemed to be better than ever.

FAMOUS PLAYERS

The 1915–1916 filmmaking season started early—on the last day of August at the most sweltering time of year. Many of St. Augustine's residents had fled to cooler locations, and the whole town routinely shut down for a half-day holiday on Thursday afternoons since so little business was being transacted in local stores. However, the Famous Players Film Company had decided to produce a moving picture version of the novel and play *Bella Donna,* which required an Egyptian setting. The company put out press releases saying that it had planned on going to Egypt to make the film, but the war in Europe had prevented travel. Whether or not this was true, Famous Players declared, "The sandy wastes of Florida, however, have made an admirable substitute for the African backgrounds."[1]

The players and cameramen registered at the Monson Hotel on the bayfront, one of the few hotels that remained open year-round. The film's directors, Hugh Ford and Edwin S. Porter, brought along their wives.[2] Porter had already established himself as one of the most important directors of the early silent era. He had directed *The Great Train Robbery* for Edison in 1903 and pioneered in developing motion pictures as a narrative form. Porter had started his career as a cameraman, and his films were noted for their clever use of the camera to create scenes. (Eventually he would quit directing and return to doing technical work with cameras.)

The leading lady of the company was Pauline Frederick, who brought her mother with her. She had already earned fame as an actress on Broadway and would become one of the best-known motion picture actresses of her day. In 1915 she was at the start of her film career, and Famous Players had recently signed her to a long-term contract. Frederick possessed a startling, dark beauty that suited her for strong female roles.

In *Bella Donna* Frederick plays a ruthless, ambitious woman who is slowly poisoning her husband, Thomas Holding. Famous Players advertised her as "alluring and treacherous . . . the Serpent of the Nile." The Villa Flora, which had been used just months earlier in Fox's *The Devil's Daughter*, was used extensively, while desert scenes were taken on the dunes of Anastasia Island. At the film's conclusion the malevolent Frederick, her murder plot foiled, dies of disappointment in the desert.[3]

Heavy summer thunderstorms drove the moviemakers indoors some days, slowing down production, but this may actually have been a lucky thing since the Famous Players studio and offices—located on the upper floors of a building in New York City—were gutted by fire just two days after the travelers returned from Florida. Fortunately, the cans of unedited film were still stored in a fireproof vault when the fire broke out. Because of the delays the film did not premiere until November.

When he returned to New York City, director Porter gave an extended statement to the *New York Times*, putting a humorous twist on the company's Florida sojourn:

> I am afraid that, despite the many personal friends which we made during our stay in St. Augustine, the old town heaved a metaphorical sigh of relief when we departed. Before we finished it would have been hard for a native son returning home from a two weeks' vacation to have recognized his old home town.

Of course, we were after Egyptian and Oriental atmosphere, and when we failed to find it we went right ahead and made it. As a result, Moorish kiosks sprang up overnight, and side streets which had been slumbering peacefully for half a century suddenly found themselves buried under the greatest sandstorm that ever swept Florida.

Crowds of natives stood about and watched us bury the pavements under cartloads of sands, for we had to have a Moorish village and the pavements of St. Augustine are not calculated to increase the illusion of Orientalism. Having obliterated all traces of the paving contractor's handicraft, we then bribed several energetic youngsters to capture all the scrawny, half-starved looking dogs they could lay their hands on— for an Oriental village must have its quota of many mongrels.

After we had constructed our village, there remained one blot on the landscape in the form of a signpost on one of the street corners. That corner must be in the picture, so there was nothing to do but to temporarily remove the post. This we did, but in replacing it we inadvertently turned the post around. As a result one convivial soul who was returning at a very early hour in the morning, after consulting the signpost most laboriously, entered a house four doors down the wrong street and was ejected by a very irate husband.[4]

EQUITABLE

Early in October a company of players from Equitable Films, with Webster Cullison as their leader, checked in at the Monson Hotel. They were making scenes for a picture based on the novel *Idols* by English writer William J. Locke, and St. Augustine was to stand in for Monte Carlo. The lead actress was Katharine Kaelred, a noted stage performer who had played "the original vamp" in the Broadway stage production of *A Fool There Was*. Equitable would later claim that the exterior shots had been made in French Martinique, but their crew may have gotten no farther south than St. Augustine. The *St. Augustine Record* reported that Cullison liked the town so well he asked Equitable to send down a second troupe to make another film.[5]

In late November that second contingent arrived to record exterior settlings for *Her Great Hour*, the story of a working girl named Nan Perrine,

Two actors from *Her Great Hour*, probably Molly McIntyre and Richard Lynn, sit on the loggia in the Hotel Ponce de Leon courtyard. (From *Moving Picture World*)

played by Molly McIntyre. Stanner E. V. Taylor wrote the screenplay and directed the action. One scene representing high society was staged on the loggia of the Hotel Ponce de Leon and was recorded at night under brilliant lights. This provided an impressive new display for St. Augustine spectators, who watched the action from King Street in front of the hotel. When the motion picture came out, one reviewer dismissed it as the usual collection of contrived plot twists, but added, "The semi-tropical vegetation of California, or Florida, or wherever the pictures were taken, is combined with ancient fortifications which are viewed in vistas of immensity and present a charming glimpse of unusual landscape."[6]

KALEM

In November 1915 the Kalem Company, old hands at filmmaking in St. Augustine, drove down over the new brick road from Jacksonville in a seven-passenger "machine" and a Ford truck to take some exterior shots for *The Lotus Woman*. After collecting some film footage and scouting the fort, the fire ruins, and the Peck House on St. George Street, they returned to their studio in Jacksonville that evening. The next week they returned to take some more "special scenes," and a week after that they came back for a longer stay. Director Harry Millarde and Alice Hollister were among those who took rooms at the Monson.[7]

A reporter for the *St. Augustine Record* reported the good news that "members of the motion picture companies operating here are out today, some of them attired in military uniform, and attracting much attention." St. Augustine seems to have suited Kalem's motion picture drama. A reviewer of the completed film declared, "Harry Millarde, in executing his duties as director, has seen to it that a convincing atmosphere has been obtained. The supposed locale is an anonymous Latin-American country; and settings, costumes, and scenery realistically lay emphasis on this illusion." A second commentator agreed: "The unusual atmosphere of the story is greatly enhanced by the seventeenth century background of St. Augustine and its historic forts."[8]

Alice Hollister, whom Kalem touted as "the original screen vampire," plays the lead role as the Lotus Woman, a Latin temptress. In this "perfect whirlwind of melodramatic action" involving war and love, Hollister ultimately succumbs in the expected moral finale by committing suicide.[9] Theda Bara had proven such a marketable product for Fox that almost every film company seemingly wanted a "vamp" in their stable of players.

MUTUAL FILM CORPORATION

The Monson Hotel was a busy place in the early winter of 1915. Next to take up residence there was Ormi Hawley, a familiar face to St. Augustinians from her days with Lubin. She had now joined Mutual Film Corporation. Hawley and the Mutual crew spent less than a week in town, however, getting atmospheric settings for the movie *Her American Prince*, which was set in a mythical European kingdom. The play is a comedy of mistaken identities in which Bradley Barker plays the roles of both "the prince" to Hawley's "princess" and an American physician who is mistaken for the prince.[10]

Having completed *Bella Donna* back in September, the Famous Players returned to St. Augustine in early December and were able to take rooms in the more upscale Hotel Alcazar, now open for the season. Sidney Olcott, director of *The Moth and the Flame,* led the contingent. Hazel Dawn (accompanied by her mother) and on-screen mature matron Dora Mills Adams were the leading ladies of the group. The photoplay, *My Lady Incog.,* combines suspense with comedy as Dawn disguises herself as a rich European baroness in an attempt to catch jewel thieves who prey upon the wealthy patrons of resort hotels—the Hotel Ponce de Leon serving, appropriately, as the high-toned resort hotel.[11]

As usual, the reviews were kinder to the cinematography than to the storyline. "More effective lighting and photography in all probability has never been obtained," wrote the reviewer for *Motography.* "The exterior scenes were produced in Florida. Mr. Olcott used only the most appropriate and choice locations in that land, it seems."[12] When the movie came to town, the Jefferson Theatre invited locals to come and see the film they had witnessed in production. "It is said that some exceedingly pretty views of St. Augustine are worked into the play and as there are hundreds now in the city who saw the scenes as they were enacted for the motion picture camera, they will want to see the results on the screen."[13]

The day after Olcott's band returned to their Jacksonville winter quarters, Robert Vignola brought another Famous Players company to St. Augustine direct from New York. Pauline Frederick was once again, as in *Bella Donna,* called upon to play a powerful female lead—actually two, since she acts as both mother and daughter in the drama *The Spider.* In a convoluted scenario, Frederick becomes entangled in a web of deceit. At the beginning of the story she is a poor girl who runs away to Europe with a rich nobleman, leaving her own little daughter behind. Years later the nobleman kidnaps a young woman, who kills him. At this point Frederick recognizes the young murderer as her own long-lost daughter. To save her daughter from execution, Frederick takes her place.[14]

At the very end of 1915 the Metro Company came to St. Augustine to take scenes in the "everglades" (as the motion picture magazines imagined all of rural Florida to be). Mary Miles Minter, star of the previous year's *Always in the Way*, and her mother Charlotte Shelby, would again play key roles in the drama *Dimples*. The story begins in a tumbledown tenement in some northern city where Mary lives with her aged father. The only joy in the life of her waif character is a rag doll that becomes the hiding place of a fortune in paper money when her miserly father dies. Mary is sent to live in the South with an aunt (played by her mother) and is followed by a thief who knows the secret contents of the doll. The doll becomes the thin thread that holds the story together. In the end the fortune is revealed, just in time to bail a young man out of financial difficulties. Of course, Mary and the young man decide to combine their financial resources and their lives at the conclusion of the movie.[15]

Minter had now turned fourteen years old and soon would be demanding more substantial roles as a grown woman, although her greatest asset remained her girlish charm. She would continue to be in great demand, making several movies each year and coming to rival Mary Pickford as "America's Sweetheart." In early 1922 her most recent director, William Desmond Taylor, was murdered in his home near Los Angeles. Although no one was ever charged with the crime, Minter was suspected of being somehow involved. Coming quickly on the heels of comedian Fatty Arbuckle's sensational trial in the death of a young woman during a party at Arbuckle's home, the rumors ended Minter's career. She lived in comfortable retirement to become a charming little old lady that few people realized had once been one of America's greatest female movie stars.

In mid-January another Metro troupe, headed by Marguerite Snow with her personal maid, checked in at the Hotel Ponce de Leon. This was a big step up in accommodations from Snow's 1912 visit with Thanhouser, when she and her company had stayed across the street in the modest Granada Hotel. They remained at the Ponce de Leon only long enough to shoot some scenes on the hotel grounds (and perhaps at nearby locations) for a motion picture entitled *A Corner in Cotton*. This movie was set in New York and Savannah, but for some reason Metro decided to take a few scenes in St. Augustine.[16]

GAUMONT MOTION PICTURE COMPANY

In the fall of 1915 the Gaumont Company, an established French film distribution firm that had recently set up a studio in New York, leased the Dixieland Theatre in South Jacksonville where so many other movie companies had produced films. When St. Augustine's Chamber of Commerce learned of Gaumont's intentions to come south, their secretary wrote a letter inviting the group to visit St. Augustine. The Chamber of Commerce exhorted the local citizens to be good hosts to the motion picture people. Saying that the moviemakers liked what the Ancient City had to offer but had complained that stores in town did not carry enough stock, the chamber also warned businessmen not to take advantage of the visitors by overcharging—supposedly the reason why Los Angeles was losing patronage.[17]

In early January director Henri Vernot and a small group of players from Gaumont registered at the Hotel Alcazar. Marguerite Courtot and Sydney Mason were the lead actors in a troupe making *The Dead Alive*. They took at least one scene in the courtyard of the Hotel Ponce de Leon, but evidently most of the film was made in Jacksonville. Courtot—partly through trick photography—plays the roles of twin sisters. One sister marries a millionaire but falls off his yacht and drowns. Later a disreputable gambling house owner who possesses the power of hypnotism induces the other sister to impersonate the miraculously restored wife. Eventually, the gambler's plot is revealed and the millionaire marries the twin sister of the wife he lost. In the film the Hotel Ponce de Leon furnishes an elegant backdrop for the millionaire to inhabit.[18]

Gaumont's next project required fifty actors, one hundred local extras, and a menagerie of animals from a traveling circus that had stopped in St. Augustine. *The Haunted Manor* is set in India and America, with St. Augustine portraying both locales. Fort Marion's courtyard provided an Oriental arena for a throng including English soldiers and Indian rajahs. "Arabs, Turks, negroes and East Indians are there in abundance," explained the *St. Augustine Record*. Local men and women, both white and black, supplied the quota of Englishmen and Indians. Edwin Middleton, the film's director, told *Motion Picture News*, "The rights to use the main thoroughfare of the picturesque city were granted . . . and a big parade, a feature of the story, was photographed." Camels, elephants, and donkeys from the circus participated in the spectacle.[19]

When the movie was released it received poor reviews for the coherence of its plot but high marks for the Florida scenery. *Motion Picture News* commented, "The scene ultimately shifts to America. For these scenes the players go to St. Augustine for settings amid the fashionable surroundings of the winter colony."[20]

In *The Haunted Manor* Iva Shepard plays an American girl who mistakenly thinks she has killed an Indian rajah, flees to the United States, marries, fakes her own death, hides in a hidden chamber in a manor house, and finally is obliged to come out of hiding because the police think her husband has murdered her—when it also is revealed that she actually did not kill anyone back in India at the beginning of the film.[21]

Gaumont was well known for its travelogue shorts, and as the crew worked in St. Augustine, they made a half-reel addition to their "See America First" series. *Historic St. Augustine, Florida,* featured "curious Spanish types of architecture," including "the oldest house in the United States," as well as "golden sunshine" and beach scenes.[22] While the Gaumont folks were taking scenes around town, H. B. Aldrich, manager of the Orpheum Theatre, paid them to film the unveiling ceremony of a bronze statue of Henry M. Flagler at the railway station. The moving picture captured many of the men, women, and children from the community who participated in the ceremony. A few days later Aldrich was able to show the film to his neighbors over four days in a row, and in March he revived it for another two days.[23] Today, that statue of Henry Flagler is a conspicuous landmark that has been relocated to the front gateway of Flagler College, the former Hotel Ponce de Leon, which served as a setting for so many silent movies in former years.

The St. Augustine Chamber of Commerce established a committee to correspond with northern movie companies, with the goal of enticing them to visit St. Augustine and perhaps establish a year-round presence in the city. The *St. Augustine Record* ran an editorial explaining that Gaumont had come to town, at least in part, because the company had advertised its

James Ingraham, longtime Flagler lieutenant and mayor of St. Augustine, presided over the unveiling of the statue of Henry M. Flagler. (Courtesy of the P. K. Yonge Library of Florida History, University of Florida)

desire to shoot a scene next to a waterwheel. The *Record* was able to attract Gaumont to the waterwheel at the Hood Mill on Riberia Street—the same wheel used years before in *Pearl of the Punjab*. The *Record's* editorial went on, "No other city in the United States has as much in desirable material. The ocean bay, woods, magnificent hotels, palatial homes, ancient buildings, old fort, city gates, narrow streets, beaches afford material for almost anything needed, except mountains."[24]

Although St. Augustine managed to attract the motion picture makers on a regular basis, the town was never able to land a company that would stay for more than a few months. In February 1916 the Ford Film Company of Philadelphia advanced a proposal to set up a studio in St. Augustine and make one comedy a week. However, the company wanted the city or local citizens to buy one-fifth of the company's stock. This proposal came to nothing, and perhaps it was just as well, since film production companies were forming and failing with regularity.[25]

Late January 1916 found Ormi Hawley back in St. Augustine. In the fall she had left the struggling Lubin Company, and now she was performing for Peerless, a production company that released movies through the World Film Corporation. Her troupe took some scenes at Dr. Garnett's orange grove and on the grounds of the Hotel Ponce de Leon. The film, *The Social Highwayman*, was directed by Edwin August, who also played the starring role as a high-society gentleman who invites rich people to his mansion and then, through clever stratagems, steals their valuables and donates the proceeds to the poor. *Motography's* reviewer called it a "whirlwind melodramatic offering" that required viewers to check their commonsense at the theater door. "There are trap doors, sliding mantels, secret elevators, lightning changes, clever escapes, and all the rest of the inexhaustible impossibilities that enter into such a story."[26] When *The Social Highwayman* played at the Orpheum Theatre, the advertisement induced locals to come see it with the promise of "lots of St. Augustine people taking parts. . . . See yourself on the screen."[27]

THANHOUSER

In October 1915 Thanhouser returned to Jacksonville, where the company had just erected a $30,000 glassed-roof studio that protected them from the elements and allowed filming even on days when passing showers chased actors and cameramen off outdoor stages. Edwin Thanhouser explained the logic behind investing in this new studio in an interview that epitomized the thinking of many eastern movie company executives at the time:

> Florida is practically virgin territory for motion picture purposes as compared with other regions which have earlier attracted the attention of motion picture makers. With the Florida studio as a base, we expect to make pictures up and down the coast, at Miami, Savannah, through the West Indies and Bahamas. The Jacksonville studio is located near the center of things there, yet it is in easy range of desirable outside locations. It is a point of considerable advantage to a manufacturer located in New York. It is a short run there and I can keep closely in touch

with operations there without being separated too far from the plant in New Rochelle.[28]

Edwin Thanhouser himself came down from New Rochelle to inspect the new studio, then traveled on to St. Augustine to scout locations. Work on their first production, *The Oval Diamond*, began in late December. The "detective adventure story" is set in South Africa, and St. Augustine provided some of the exotic scenery for this location. In one scene an actor drops from a tree to land on another actor in the garden of the Villa Flora.[29]

Thanhouser's second St. Augustine motion picture, *What Doris Did*, starred Doris Grey, a nineteen-year-old who had just been selected as the "prettiest girl" at a gala ball in Boston sponsored by Thanhouser and staged by theater directors. Thanhouser star Florence La Badie headed the panel of judges who selected the winner. At the time "Doris Grey" had still been using her real name, Sophie Sadowski, and had done only a little acting on a local level. However, her prize was a starring role in a film by Thanhouser, which had dreamed up the contest as a publicity stunt.[30]

Most of the interior scenes for *What Doris Did* were made at the home studio in New Rochelle, but the Thanhouser group stayed at the Monson Hotel for a while to shoot some segments in St. Augustine, including beach landscapes. The movie involves the Secret Service trying to discover foreign agents operating in the country. Interest in the Great War being fought in Europe had begun to spill over into American movies. In the film Doris is able to prove that her lover has been falsely accused and imprisoned. Grey's acting won endorsement from reviewers as "promising," and Thanhouser signed her to a contract. However, her movie career extended only to the production of seven films over the next two years.

Another release, *The Flight of the Duchess*, took full advantage of St. Augustine's historic locations. The writer for *Motion Picture News* declared: "The scenery is notable, and great care has been shown in arranging the period costumes and settings. The scenery is notable and someone has worked hard on looking up locations; they are striking and successful in interpreting the atmosphere of the picture." The movie, starring Gladys Hulette, is the story of a modern-day duke who is fascinated with the Middle Ages and demands that all his subjects dress in medieval garb. One girl refuses to go along and, in fact, spurns the duke's amorous advances to run away with a gypsy. Disillusioned at the deflation of his romantic notions, the duke orders everyone to return to normal clothes. *Motography*'s reviewer commented, "The settings which Mr. [Eugene] Nowland has supplied are indeed artistic. Seldom does one find a picture whose every scene has a background so tasteful and real."[31]

Thanhouser's final two films to use St. Augustine for some settings starred foreign-born actress Adele Freed, who was known under her husband's name as the Baroness Dewitz. She also used the stage name Madame Valkyrien. Formerly a star of the Royal Danish Ballet, Valkyrien radiated blonde Scandinavian beauty. Edwin Thanhouser came to Jacksonville to watch her perform in the studio, but *Hidden Valley* required her to venture into the "jungles" of Florida. Some scenes were taken in St. Augustine. The story is a familiar one in escapist fiction: a white women becomes a goddess and almost a sacrifice in black Africa before being rescued by a white American adventurer.[32]

In the next film, *The Image Maker of Thebes*, Valkyrien is a commoner who makes clay idols. The Egyptian pharaoh orders her killed because she fell in love with the pharaoh's son, the Prince of Tsa. The prince tries to prevent the execution, but is fatally wounded in a rescue attempt, and the girl is thrown to crocodiles. Before their respective demises the star-crossed lovers vow to meet again at the temple of Tsa. Years pass, and it is 1916. An American young man and woman meet at a resort hotel in Florida and immediately sense that they have known each other before. It turns out that the young lady is an actress who must travel to Egypt to make a motion picture. Her modern-day lover follows and, after trials and struggles, they are united (or reunited?) at the temple of Tsa, now a ruin.[33]

Thanhouser built a set for the temple of Tsa on the beach at Jacksonville, but the film company came to St. Augustine to take pictures for the modern-day ruins of the temple. The crumbling, smoke-stained, but still-standing walls of the Vedder House, which had been destroyed in the 1914 fire, served as the remains of the temple. Edison had used the still-intact Vedder House in its *A Night at the Inn* two years earlier, shortly before the fire.

The Thanhouser people said that they would be back in the fall, but within a few weeks the Metro distribution company told Thanhouser that it would no longer handle its productions. Thanhouser soon made a deal with Pathé for distribution, but circulation of Thanhouser films was drastically reduced. With its revenues severely cut, Thanhouser closed its Jacksonville studio to save costs and never returned to Florida.

SERIAL FILM COMPANY

Toward the end of the winter tourist season a small classified ad appeared in the *St. Augustine Record*, reading: "Wanted—Fifty white men of comparatively small stature for moving picture. Apply Chamber of Commerce after four o'clock this afternoon." A story elsewhere in the same issue explained that a movie company also wanted about twenty-five young white ladies and two hundred Negroes. Two days later the *Record* ran a long story explaining what these "extras" were needed for—especially the "white men of comparatively small stature" who were to portray Asians in a grand serial movie to be made in St. Augustine.[34]

William "Big Bill" Steiner had come to town to film the early episodes of a sixteen-part serial entitled *The Yellow Menace*. Steiner was a true pioneer in the film industry who had started in the business in 1896 and had found his niche making low-budget films. (He would continue working through the silent era, and his son William O. Steiner Jr. would still be making B Westerns into the 1940s.)

Steiner had no problem finding white women willing to playact, but black men came in more slowly. The boys of the Keewatin School—a small boarding school for northern boys located at the south end of town—filled in the ranks of the white men. The black men, small-statured white men, and Keewatin boys were engaged to play the Oriental "heavies" in a drama the *Record* said portrayed "the overthrow of the white race. . . . The story deals with the peril of the Orient, and pictures an invasion of the United States by hordes from China, Japan, and India." When the series premiered, advertisements billed it as "a trumpet call for preparedness against the danger from across the Pacific, against which ex-President Roosevelt has warned the country."[35]

Episode 1 of *The Yellow Menace* begins in an American compound somewhere in China. The City Gates serve as the entrance to the American

Edwin Stevens, in the guise of Ali Singh, stands in the entryway to the Hotel Ponce de Leon. (Courtesy of George Eastman Museum)

quarter, and Fort Marion functions as its defensive citadel. Edwin Stevens portrays "Ali Singh, the Mongolian Demon," who is out to conquer America. The United States is unprepared to defend itself and is distracted by the Great War in Europe. Hordes of black men, short-statured white men, and schoolboys in makeup overwhelm the defenders of Fort Marion, apparently played by the men of Company B of the Florida Militia. The Gatling guns of the militiamen serve as impressive, smoke-spewing props for the action, but their effect is to no avail against the overwhelming numbers of the foe.

William Dean Howells, once the most popular writer in America after Mark Twain, happened to be spending the winter in St. Augustine and witnessed the spectacle: "On a single occasion last year a company of three hundred combatants—white and black, men, women, and children, hired overnight for the purpose—thronged the noble place and repelled each other in an invasion by the Japanese, with a constant explosion of old-fashioned musketry which sounded like the detonations of

The American soldiers and Oriental attackers battle inside Fort Marion while spectators line the ramparts to watch the action. Note that the entrance to the chapel had been restored by 1916. (Courtesy of Castillo de San Marcos archives, National Park Service)

the unmuffled motors of a fleet of such boats as infest all our inland or coastwise waters."[36]

After this spectacular opening, the serial settles down into the small-set routine of most melodramas. No panoramic scenes of armadas from the East threaten American shores; instead, Ali Singh establishes his headquarters in an opium den in New York City's Chinatown. He hatches various plots to thwart a banker's efforts to influence the government to restrict immigration from the Orient. (In reality, immigration from China and Japan to the United States was already restricted at the time.) Margaret Gale, playing the banker's daughter, is often the damsel in peril.

By the end of the series every trapdoor escape, secret panel, poison spider, hypnotic trance, Oriental torture, car chase, airplane crash, and other set piece of melodramatic drama had been exploited. With the operations of German U-boats in the Atlantic attracting public attention, a submarine is even enlisted in the story. In the end Ali Singh escapes but, fortunately, never to reappear in any "Yellow Menace, Series 2."[37]

William Dean Howells, who confined his storytelling to the printed page, found that the motion picture actors visiting St. Augustine made an interesting sideshow for regular winter visitors. He reported in a *Harper's Magazine* article on his observations:

> St. Augustine is indeed the setting of almost any most dramatic fact, as the companies of movie-players, rehearsing their pantomimes everywhere, so recurrently testified. No week passed without the encounter of these genial fellow-creatures dismounting from motors at this picturesque point or that, or delaying in them to darken an eye, or redden a lip or cheek, or pull a bodice into shape, before alighting to take part in the drama. I talk as if there were no men in these affairs, but there were plenty, preferably villains, like brigands or smugglers or savages, with consoling cowboys or American cavalrymen for the rescue of ladies in extremity. Seeing the films so much in formation, we naturally went a great deal to see them ultimated in the movie-theaters, where we found them nearly all bad.[38]

VIM COMEDY FILM COMPANY

In mid-April Vim Comedy Film Company, a new company specializing in one-reel comedy shorts, checked in to the Keystone Hotel. Arthur Hotaling, formerly Lubin's comedy director in Jacksonville, had moved to the new company when it took over the old Yacht Club in Jacksonville. Hotaling brought in his protégé from Lubin, Oliver Hardy, and his new partner, Billy Ruge, who were teamed as "Plump and Runt." Their film *Never Again* took the Dale family to Spain for a vacation. St. Augustine, of course, played its familiar role as Spain. Pop Dale (Bert Tracy) gets into mischief along with Plump and Runt when they are infatuated with a Spanish dancer. Helen Gilmore, as Mrs. Dale, and Florence McLaughlin and Rae Godfrey, as the Dale daughters, step in to save the boys from making fools of themselves.[39]

Hardy would make sixty-five comedy shorts for Vim in Jacksonville, thirty-five of them Plump and Runt escapades. Near the end of 1916

Oliver "Babe" Hardy began his career in Jacksonville making comedy shorts. He came to St. Augustine to film the Spanish-themed *Never Again*. (From *Moving Picture World*)

A candid photo taken of some of the cast members of *Never Again* in the courtyard of the Hotel Ponce de Leon. Rae Godfrey is second from the right. (Courtesy of Randy Skretvedt)

Oliver Hardy stands in the middle of a group of Vim players amidst the ruins of an Egyptian temple—probably erected in Atlantic Beach for *The Image Maker of Thebes*. (Courtesy of Randy Sketvedt)

Hardy discovered that the managers of Vim had been skimming from the profits of the company, and Vim dissolved in recriminations. Hardy soon relocated west to Hollywood, where he would meet Stan Laurel and go on to make movie history.

STAGE STRUCK GIRLS

While the Serial Film Company managers were in town, the *St. Augustine Record* and a private promoter made a deal to run a contest the winners of which would star in a motion picture made by the Serial Company. Five young women would be selected to travel to the Serial studio in New York and make a two-reel film. The five winners would earn their way by inducing St. Augustine residents to subscribe to the *Record*—which was the newspaper's underlying aim for the contest. Existing subscribers who renewed for one or two years earned a set number of points for the girl whom the subscriber supported; new subscribers earned twice as many points as old subscribers for their favorites. The *Record* published daily tabulations showing how the leading contestants stood in the rankings— thus making it a real race.[40]

A second part of the challenge asked St. Augustine residents to submit a scenario for the two-reel movie that would be enacted by the winning contestants. The author of the best scenario would win a fifty-dollar gold piece. On May 8 the *Record* announced that this contest had been won by Ida Lewis Floyd, who also happened to be one of the leading contestants in the subscription competition.[41]

Her scenario cleverly turns the contest itself into a dramatic situation. Five "Stage Struck Girls" in the town of "Augusta" vie to win a trip to New York to make a movie. One of the girls, Anita Frederick, is an orphan living with her aunt. She is reluctant to enter the contest, but her aunt tells her, "Dear child, in your beauty lies our only hope of rescue from our poverty." While canvassing from door to door Anita chances to meet handsome, wealthy Walter Hurlburt, who is immediately smitten and corrals his friends at the yacht club into voting for Anita. Of course, Anita wins and goes to New York with her friends, where she impresses the movie director so favorably that he offers her a contract to star in the movies. Walter has followed the stage-struck girls to New York and professes his love for Anita. Thus, she must decide between a career in motion pictures and life with Walter in Augusta. Anita chooses Walter.[42]

The circulation contest ended on May 15, and the *Record* claimed to have added six hundred new subscribers through the promotion. The five winners, Edyth Corbett, Ida Lewis Floyd, Rebecca Botkowsky, Gretchen Oldfather, and Ruth Moeller—along with a chaperone—were soon on their way to New York on a Clyde Line steamer from Jacksonville. Ida Lewis Floyd continued to be the writer in the group, sending letters home for publication in the *Record*. Gretchen Oldfather, "an extremely pretty girl of the blonde type," caught the eye of a "tall, dark officer of the ship," according to Floyd. Gretchen also sang in the music room for the pleasure of her fellow travelers. When their ship reached New York, Bill Steiner of the Serial Company was on the dock waiting to greet them.[43]

The St. Augustine girls seem to have done the town up right. They ate lobster in their hotel, attended several live plays and a couple of movies, went shopping at Macy's, visited Grant's tomb, rode the subway, went on the thrill rides at Coney Island, and were taken back-stage at the extravagant Hippodrome Theatre. Once the filming got underway, the aspiring actresses took the ferry to Fort Lee, New Jersey, where interior shots were

The stars of *Stage Struck Girls* prepare to depart for New York with their chaperone, Mrs. R. B. Jarvis. *From the left*: Gretchen Oldfather (*front*), Edyth Klair Corbett, Ida Lewis Floyd, Rebecca Botkowsky, and Ruth Moeller. (From *St. Augustine Record*)

taken in a studio. Then they motored to a Hudson River estate for exterior scenes. Other venues for picture-taking included standard sites visitors to New York typically visit: the Flatiron Building, Washington Square, and the New York Public Library.[44]

Stage Struck Girls premiered at the Orpheum on the morning of June 21 in a test run before some of the girls and a *Record* reporter. The newspaper declared it "bright, snappy and all merit. . . . The girls act like professionals, and it is difficult to believe that they had no former experience as movie actresses. Everyone in St. Augustine will want to see the play, many will want to see it twice or more. It is good and will bear repetition." The Orpheum raised its admission prices by a nickel to ten and twenty cents to cover the cost of producing the film, and after being shown in town for a week the movie was sent to theaters around the state. Gretchen Oldfather's blonde good looks had earned her the role of the orphan girl Anita, but in real life she did not marry a rich yachtsman; instead, she found a mate in Clarence Philips, an office clerk at the Florida East Coast Railway headquarters.[45]

Not everyone in town took to the movies like the Stage Struck Girls. An editorial in the *St. Augustine Record* reflected a common criticism, saying that motion pictures appealed "to the baser passion of human nature." It asked that local theater managers screen "only the best productions." This attitude of disapproval took solid form in a movement, led by some clergymen, to close theaters on Sundays. Florida's "blue law" required that all businesses, save for a few such as drugstores, remain closed on Sunday, but this law was seldom enforced and singling out the theaters for special treatment would raise the ire of other businessmen who traded on Sunday and feared they might be the next target. After a while the controversy passed and the theaters remained open.[46]

Hostility to the movies had more serious consequences in Jacksonville in 1916. That January the Equitable Film Company's cameramen filmed a "mob scene" on a city street that—too realistically—destroyed a brick building and a saloon while uniformed policemen flailed away at rioters with fake billy clubs. The local newspaper editorialized that this celluloid depiction of violence lowered the moral order of the city and questioned whether the financial gains flowing from the movie people outweighed the disturbance to civil society. The mayoral election that followed pitted a pro-movie candidate against an anti-movie candidate—and the latter won.[47] With the welcome mat removed by the mayor, Jacksonville's reign as the winter film capital of America waned and, meanwhile, the steady drift of major studios to Hollywood gained momentum.

6

LEADING LADIES TAKE CENTER STAGE

1917

Having enjoyed a very successful moviemaking season in 1915–1916, the people of St. Augustine expected another excellent crop of productions with the coming of the cool-weather months. The *St. Augustine Record* predicted, "St. Augustine is destined to become a great motion picture city, and each day more about the advantages of the Ancient City is learned by the screen people."[1]

The efforts of the chamber of commerce and St. Augustine's city government to attract movie companies to St. Augustine paid off in the late fall of 1916 when the Herbert Brenon Film Corporation decided to produce a major film in town. Brenon, an experienced and highly respected movie director, had just broken with William Fox over the degree of control Brenon would have over films he produced for Fox. Brenon's new partner was Lewis J. Selznick, the father of David O. Selznick of *Gone with the Wind* fame. When Brenon and a company of twenty actors and technicians arrived at St. Augustine's railroad station, several town councilmen and members of the chamber of commerce were on hand to welcome them.[2]

Brenon's play was *Lucrezia Borgia,* based on a drama by Victor Hugo. However, Brenon decided to change the name to *The Eternal Sin* when he realized that few people had any idea who Lucrezia Borgia had been. Florence Reed, a noted Broadway actress, would play the leading role in her

Vandals remove the "B" from the "Borgia" coat of arms, and Florence Reed discovers that it now reads "orgia"—or "orgy." For *The Eternal Sin* moviemakers affixed the plaque to the courtyard wall of the Hotel Ponce de Leon. (From *Motion Picture Magazine*)

movie debut, while the Hotel Ponce de Leon would play the part of the Borgia palace. The moviemakers spent two weeks in St. Augustine, shooting one hundred different scenes. The play is one of an unhappy marriage, palace intrigue, and a long-lost son (played by Richard Barthelmess). Hugo had presented Lucrezia sympathetically, as does the movie, but she manages inadvertently to poison her own son, who kills her as he is dying.

The reviewer for *Moving Picture World* gave St. Augustine its usual high marks as an authentic setting: "The scenes were taken in Florida, the courtyards and interiors of some of the most famous of its hotels serving admirably for Italy in the fourteenth century." Most interior scenes were made on an elaborately constructed set in New York.[3]

Florence Reed, who had been born into a theater family, continued acting in live performances on stage, made silent movies, successfully transitioned to talking movies, and ended her career with appearances on television. Herbert Brenon made several motion pictures on a monumental scale during the next decade and a half but, unfortunately for his reputation today, most have not survived.

NORMA TALMADGE FILM CORPORATION

Along with Florence Reed, who enjoyed one of the longest careers in cinema, Norma Talmadge ranked as one of the most accomplished and popular stars of the silent era. She had begun in movies with Vitagraph in 1910, but her career took off when she married movie exhibitor Joseph M. Schenck in October 1916 and together they formed the Norma Talmadge Film Corporation. He supplied the capital, and she supplied the talent. They established their company headquarters in New York City, but that winter they came to Jacksonville to make their second film, *The Law of Compensation*.

Like so many of Talmadge's films, the story is a melodrama of contemporary life for a young woman. In this case a bored and neglected wife with a young child is tempted to run away with a flimflam artist who promises to make her a star vocalist on the New York stage. Fortunately, her father realizes the danger and recounts to his daughter the woeful story of how her mother had deserted her family to run away with a smooth-talking conman and had died in regret at her folly. Warned in time, the young wife

The advertisement for *Redemption* emphasizes the names of Nesbit and Thaw since they were notorious from the "murder of the century." (From *Motion Picture News*)

remains with her husband and child. Talmadge plays the parts of both mother (in a long flashback) and daughter.

The Law of Compensation opens with an extended episode at a girls' boarding school. Talmadge's company drove down from Jacksonville in a caravan of eight large touring cars to St. Augustine's state School for the Deaf and Blind in order to film this portion of the story. The girls' basketball team played a game that became part of the movie. They may have made some other scenes while in town, since the *St. Augustine Record* later claimed, "Many of the scenes were made right here in St. Augustine."[4]

Two of Talmadge's directors, Joseph A. Golden and Julius Steger, created the new company Triumph Films, and Joseph Schenck made an agreement with them to produce a film in Jacksonville. Two of the actresses from *The Law of Compensation* would join the cast, but the main attraction would be the famous Evelyn Nesbit, one of the leading characters in the young century's most dramatic real-life melodrama: Harry Thaw's murder of Stanford White.

Nesbit had been discovered as a young salesgirl in Wanamaker's department store in Philadelphia and soon moved to New York City, where she became one of the most popular models for artists and photographers. Her face became widely known on the covers of women's magazines, in advertisements, and on postcards. Charles Dana Gibson drew her as one of his "Gibson Girls." She moved to the stage as a chorus girl and then as a featured singer and dancer. The wealthy, socially well-connected architect Stanford White took her under his wing, appearing to be a fatherly patron, but according to Nesbit's later testimony, he seduced her in his lavish apartment. Pursued by several men, including John Barrymore, she finally married the mentally unstable millionaire Harry Thaw in 1905. A year later Thaw shot and killed White in a rooftop dinner theater atop Madison Square Garden. The ensuing trial raised a frenzy in the newspapers since it involved one well-known rich man murdering another because of a beautiful woman. Thaw was found not guilty of murder by reason of insanity and was situated comfortably in an asylum.

Abandoned by the Thaw family after the trial, Nesbit made a living on the vaudeville stage. People came to her performances partly out of curiosity about the infamous woman from the Crime of the Century. Although she had appeared in three movie shorts over the years, the motion picture she made for Triumph Films in 1917 would be her first appearance as an actress in a full-length movie. Entitled *Redemption,* the movie openly exploits circumstances and characters from her life: a young chorus girl is seduced by a rich architect, but later settles down with a respectable husband, a draftsman. They have a son, played in the film by Nesbit's actual son, five-year-old Russell Thaw. The powerful, lustful architect reappears, attempts to renew his relationship with the woman and, when scorned, causes the husband to lose his job, sicken, and die. Nesbit's character survives, opens a dressmaking shop, and lives a quiet life for years until, by chance, her grown son falls in love with the malevolent architect's daughter. Ultimately, love overcomes all barriers.

The film attracted attention because of the lead actress's name, but reviewers praised it. *Moving Picture World* said, "The picture's greatest asset, however, is the unexpected force of Evelyn Nesbit's acting. She has the personality, grace, and intelligence required, and also a surprising degree of the rudiments of screen art."[5] She would go on to star in a total of eleven silent films.

Unfortunately, no copies of *Redemption* are known to exist, and, although the film is credited to St. Augustine, the extent of local exterior scenes is unknown.[6] The interiors were probably shot in a studio in Jacksonville. Interestingly, Stanford White had been a close friend of fellow architect Thomas Hastings, the designer of Henry Flagler's hotels and churches in St. Augustine.

METRO/COLUMBIA PICTURES CORPORATION

Most stars of the silent screen, such as Florence Reed and Norma Talmadge, have largely been forgotten today, but the same cannot be said of Ethel Barrymore, whose name still resonates today in large part because of the fame of her extended theater family—brothers Lionel and John and grand-niece Drew Barrymore. Born to parents who both were actors, Ethel took to the stage as a youngster. In 1895, at the age of sixteen, she appeared on Broadway with her uncle Sidney Drew (who would later direct and star in *A Florida Enchantment*). Although she loved performing before live audiences, she could not resist the possibilities of the silver screen, and made her first movie in 1914.

Thirty-seven-year-old Ethel Barrymore managed to portray a young woman in this publicity photo taken for *The Call of Her People*. (Courtesy of George Eastman Museum)

When Barrymore came to St. Augustine in 1917, she was a thirty-seven-year-old mother of three children and was losing the delicate, pretty appearance that had won her fame on the stage. The film was based on the Edward Sheldon play *Egypt*, but the movie title became *The Call of Her People*. At the beginning of the screenplay she had to portray a young gypsy girl known as "Egypt." Although *Moving Picture World* credited her "rugged personality" with making the exotic young woman believable, other reviewers opined she was too old to be playing girlish roles. In the movie, Egypt is sold by her foster father to a wealthy southern planter. She falls in love with a man from the local gentry, played by William B. Davidson (who would make hundreds of films until his death in 1947). Her gypsy lover, portrayed by Robert Whittier, follows her and murders a man. Ultimately, Barrymore heeds "the call of her people," and the two gypsy lovers flee to live a life of wandering on the open road.[7]

The Metro company used Kirkside, the home of Henry M. Flagler, as the white-columned mansion of the southern gentleman. Flagler had

In *The Call of Her People* Ethel Barrymore must choose, on her wedding day, between the rich southern gentleman William B. Davidson and the gypsy prince Robert Whittier. The drama plays out on the front porch of Kirkside, Henry M. Flagler's home beside Memorial Presbyterian Church. (Courtesy of New York Public Library)

passed away nearly four years earlier, but Barrymore may previously have met him and his wife, Mary Lily, at Greenbriar resort in West Virginia, where she and the Flaglers sometimes vacationed. The film company used the lawn and even shot some interior scenes in the house, perhaps with Mary Lily's permission. One of Flagler's closest personal friends, Dr. Andrew Anderson, entertained Barrymore at his nearby home, Markland, one evening. (Anderson had earlier allowed the grounds of Markland to be used as the setting for several films.) During the visit Barrymore lost a string of small smoky pearls. A search of every corner of the house failed to turn up the missing jewelry. Only months later when a piece of furniture was being refinished were the pearls discovered, slipped into a groove.[8]

Viola Dana, one of Metro's leading stars, came to join the Jacksonville company with her husband, director John H. Collins. Born in Brooklyn in 1897 as Virginia Flugrath, she stepped on the stage as a child actress, abandoning her given name. She started making films in 1910 and would become one of the most prolific performers of the silent era. Her sprightly personality and cute face suited her for roles in light comedies. In and around Jacksonville she made *God's Law and Man's*, in which she plays a "Hindoo" girl who marries an Englishman to escape being made a human sacrifice. She reprises a Hindoo role in *Lady Barnacle*, playing the daughter of an Indian maharajah who schemes to leave India to join her lover in America. In both movies Florida landscapes serve as India, with

Some scenes of *The Call of Her People* were shot inside Kirkside, giving us the only known early images from the interiors of Henry Flagler's home. (From *Photoplay* magazine)

Viola Dana plays an Indian girl in *God's Law and Man's*. A typical Florida landscape stands in for India, even though cabbage palms do not grow there. (From the author's collection)

the Hotel Ponce de Leon appearing as the maharajah's palace in the latter film. Each day Dana made the commute from Jacksonville to shoot the day's scenes. In *Lady Barnacle* the young Indian lady becomes a "barnacle" when she attaches herself to a stiff, puritanical young Bostonian man and sticks with him as he returns to Beacon Hill society—leading to an assortment of comedic episodes stemming from conflicting manners, morals, and misunderstandings.[9]

Another Metro performer who came to St. Augustine from Metro's southern studio in Jacksonville was Emmy Wehlen, a popular performer in musicals on stage who had ventured into the movies. She was joined by George Stuart Christie, who had a similar background on the live stage and was trying his hand at the movies for the first time. In their film, *The Duchess of Doubt*, Wehlen plays a poor girl who enters the elite winter society in St. Augustine knowing a smattering of French and pretending to be a duchess traveling incognito. She meets Christie, who is a rich man pretending to be a humble tradesman. The story is an excuse for Wehlen to waltz among wealthy socialites (played by actual hotel guests) in a selection of stunning gowns from New York designers. In reality, she did stay as a guest at the Hotel Alcazar. That hotel, along with the Ponce de Leon, Fort Marion, and the beach provided settings for her movie.[10]

Among the Metro players staying at the Bennett Hotel was Frank Currier, who recalled that he had first come to St. Augustine in 1872 with a troupe of traveling players to perform a play by Shakespeare. At that time he had stayed in the St. Augustine Hotel, which had burned to the ground in 1887 and taken a whole block of the city with it. As he aged Currier became a favorite character actor for distinguished older gentleman roles. Sixty years old in 1917, Currier played an elderly Frenchman in *The Duchess of Doubt*. He is credited with appearing in 133 films prior to his death in 1928 due to a freak accident of blood poisoning.[11]

B. S. MOSS PHOTOPLAYS

Director Ben Goetz brought a small company of fifteen or twenty players to St. Augustine and took rooms at the Monson on the bayfront. They came to stage a drama written by William O. Hurst specifically with St. Augustine in mind as the setting. His play, *In the Hands of the Law*, is a "social issue" film about the problem of miscarriages of justice in court trials when the accused are convicted on the basis of "circumstantial evidence." Lois Meredith is the female lead, and her lover is Eugene Strong. Meredith would never become a first-rank star, but her career in movies and later radio would extend through the 1930s. The movie appears not to have sparked the debate that its creators hoped for, and it passed through movie houses that year without much notice.[12]

A publicity release from the Moss company stressed the authenticity of the film's settings, explaining that the prison scenes were made in the federal prison in Atlanta, Georgia. As the release explained, "Studio sets are easily penetrated by the discerning public in this late day of motion picture education, and B. S. Moss, fully alive to the fact that realism is the order of the day, not only cast his outdoor scenes in St. Augustine, Fla., which is considered one of the beauty spots of the world, but most of the interior scenes as well were taken from the real subject."[13]

Jesse L. Lasky/Paramount

In late January, while the Metro Film Company was still working on Barrymore's gypsy movie, the Metro managers brought a second large troupe of actors to St. Augustine for an Italian movie. The leading lady of the story was "Mademoiselle" Olga Petrova, a fascinating Russian actress who had performed in Paris, Brussels, and London—or so it was said. Actually she had been born Muriel Harding in England and had enjoyed only modest success as a singer and actress on stage until she decided to adopt the intriguing stage name Olga Petrova. Company co-owner H. B. Harris, partner of Jesse L. Lasky, had discovered her in England, and Lasky brought her to the United States where she performed on stage.

In 1914 the manager of Popular Plays and Players company—which released through Metro—signed her to a motion picture contract—although Petrova, as she later claimed, had never even sat through a movie before this. Her introduction to the movies disappointed her in the roles given to female players. Women were not depicted realistically, she thought. They were either vampires or "simple, weak-brained, weak-armed maidens." She argued, "There was a place for the intelligent, resourceful, self-supporting women, as there was for the vampire, the magdalene, the betrayed innocent, the sweet and ringleted ingénue." Hence she began writing her own scenarios.[14]

Petrova also designed much of her own wardrobe. She knew that most of her audience were women and girls, and that they wanted to see stylish clothing. An actress could not wear the same dress in two different movies because her fans would remember its previous appearance. Thus, actresses were required to acquire a huge wardrobe. Petrova worked with two dress designers in New York City to make gowns that she felt flattered her figure.[15]

Her St. Augustine movie, the dramatically named *To the Death*, had been written by Petrova herself and aspired to grand spectacle. Local men, women, and children were recruited to play the parts of Italian peasants, and some of the usual St. Augustine locations were used as stages for the action: Fort Marion, the W. A. Knight residence on Oneida Street, and "Whitney's Old House," a tourist attraction on Hospital (now Aviles)

Street. In a story of "Corsican revenge," Petrova is a simple lace maker who ventures to Paris to study art and falls in love with a secret policeman. Deceived into thinking her lover has murdered her sister, Petrova stabs him in revenge. *Moving Picture World* thought the drama should have ended there, but Petrova adds a happy ending with the policeman surviving and all deceit swept away.[16] This movie would be among the last ones she would make for Popular Plays.

While the moviemakers were plying their trade in St. Augustine, the world's most respected stage actress Sarah Bernhardt stopped in town on her nationwide farewell tour. She was seventy-three years old and one of her legs had been amputated, yet she carried on like a trouper. Rather than check in to local hotels, she lived in her own comfortable private railway car. For her appearance the Jefferson Theatre was decorated with French and American flags, and the performance began with the singing of the French and U.S. national anthems. In one respect her tour was intended to raise American support for France in the Great War in Europe. She performed scenes from three plays, some in French and some in English. Her efforts brought a standing ovation.[17]

When Bernhardt's tour reached Jacksonville, Petrova attended her performance. At the time Petrova was finishing a movie in Jacksonville for Popular Plays. Afterward, Bernhardt's manager approached Petrova in the theater and asked her to come backstage to Bernhardt's dressing room. Petrova was humbled to be granted this meeting and remarked that Bernhardt was one of the few people she had ever met with truly "magnetic attraction."[18]

Although Petrova still worked for Popular Plays, she was just finishing out the terms of her contract. She had already signed a new contract with her old associate Jesse L. Lasky. By this time Petrova had risen to be one of the ranking stars of the screen, and her contract with Lasky paid her $160,000 a year.[19] For some time Petrova had felt that the motion pictures produced by Popular Plays simply lacked the quality of other companies' productions. She admired director Maurice Tourneur and was pleased to work with him at Lasky.

Tourneur ranks today as one of the most accomplished directors of the silent era. Born in France, he began his career as an artist then as an interior decorator, learning skills that served him well when he came to

America and emerged as a movie producer and director. His films were noted for the artistic composition of scenes and dramatic use of lighting effects.

On April 2 Petrova returned to St. Augustine as a Lasky employee and checked in to the luxurious Hotel Ponce de Leon. Most of the other actors and technicians, along with the four dancers in the party, found more modest accommodations.

The day that Petrova arrived in St. Augustine President Woodrow Wilson went before a joint session of Congress to ask for a declaration of war against Germany. The war had already been going on in Europe for more than two and a half years, and Americans had been preparing for the United States to enter it for a long time. St. Augustine's Catholic Club held a fund-raiser to benefit the Red Cross at the Jefferson Theatre, which was decorated with American and Red Cross flags. The young women of the club, dressed as Red Cross nurses, acted as ushers. The minister of the Presbyterian church gave an address on the importance of supporting the effort. Petrova, whose appearance had been advertised as the highlight of the evening, sang a love song, gave a dramatic sketch illustrating the range of her acting expression, then recited a poem she had written herself. The event concluded when the audience rose and sang the *Star Spangled Banner*.[20]

The *St. Augustine Record* explained the reason for Petrova's presence in St. Augustine: "This is to be an Egyptian picture, hence the reason for coming to St. Augustine to secure the proper Oriental settings."[21] In *The Undying Flame* Petrova achieved her wish to work with director Maurice Tourneur. She plays dual roles as the daughter of a pharaoh and the daughter of a modern English army officer. A scarab ring, broken in two by a pair of lovers from long ago, connects with another couple in modern times when they discover that each possesses half of that scarab ring. Local boys were recruited to play "Arabs," while the men of St. Augustine's militia unit acted as British soldiers.[22]

When *The Undying Flame* appeared at the Jefferson Theatre two months later the auditorium was packed to the rafters. Before showing the film, the theater flashed a card on the screen reading, "In a message just received by the management, Madame Petrova sends her personal greetings to you tonight." The *St. Augustine Record*, always looking for ways to boost

THE JESSE L. LASKY FEATURE PLAY CO. INC.
"*A Paramount Picture*"

MADAME PETROVA
IN
"THE UNDYING FLAME"
© 1917

PAGE IMPRESSES GRACE

Olga Petrova (*center*) is flanked by Charles Martin and Violet Reed in a scene from *The Undying Flame*. The setting is probably the palm garden of the Hotel Ponce de Leon. (From *Photofest*)

its hometown, editorialized, "St. Augustine has received an exceedingly great compliment through the way in which the beautiful local scenery and settings were worked into the picture throughout its five reels. The old fort with its ancient coquina walls, the Hotel Ponce de Leon's picturesque courtyard and our tropical palm gardens all had their share in making the splendid eastern scenes with their Oriental atmosphere."[23]

Reviews of *The Undying Flame* came in mixed. *Motion Picture News* called it "a most extraordinary production." It added, "The settings are lavish and most impressively chosen." On the other hand, *Moving Picture World* argued the studio props of ancient Egypt were too obviously faked, but St. Augustine looked like a "cleverly counterfeited" facsimile of "the land of the Pharaohs." *Motion Picture Magazine* called it "a poor picture. . . . it is produced in such a manner as to turn what was meant to be drama into laughable burlesque—over-acting in the big scenes is the simple reason."[24]

Petrova, however, liked the film very much, and she felt that Lasky and Tourneur did too. "Looking back now on the weeks spent in filming of that picture," she wrote in her autobiography, "I see it as the oasis in the desert of my cinema experiences. The film itself, aside from any share I had in it, was one that I could view with little criticism, no embarrassment, and a great deal of aesthetic pleasure."[25]

Exile, the third motion picture made by Petrova in St. Augustine that winter, again took advantage of the Ancient City's historic buildings to create a Middle Eastern ambiance. Tourneur had lived in French North Africa and knew how to replicate that atmosphere. The Jacksonville *Florida Times-Union* explained, "The company has established a veritable Arabian village in the ruins of the big fire on Charlotte and Treasury streets and here the Arabian scenes are being filmed. . . . Madame Petrova is seen in most of the pictures and her presence attracts a large audience while the celebrity and her associates are at work." Local boys and girls were recruited to play Arabs and the National Guard platoon acted as British soldiers, while a camel was shipped in by rail from Cincinnati at a cost of $400 to add a touch of realism to the scene. A day or two later the venue shifted to the courtyard of the Hotel Ponce de Leon, where high-society people gathered at a reception for the royal governor. Mrs. A. V. Monson of the Monson Hotel was cast as a "dignified and beautiful society matron." Other town notables strolled in the background as the actors went through their convolutions. Later, the action moved on to Hospital Street, and a newsman reported that the street was choked with "supers" and spectators watching the free entertainment.

> The small boy is having the time of his life frisking about in desert costume and old men with long white beards are moving about with the slow step of advanced age, dignity and wisdom. There are girls also, veiled ladies, stalwart Arabs, Nubians and soldiers. The characters of

nuns are impersonated by Mrs. Alec Canova and Mrs. Alec Solano. Negroes of all ages form a large proportion of the mob scenes and they are attired in the costumes of the Orient as are the others.[26]

The moviemakers caused a problem for local schools: boys and girls skipping classes for a chance to appear in a film drama. Parents were warned about students absconding from school and were advised to admonish their children to stay in their classrooms.[27]

When *Exile* appeared at the Jefferson Theatre in the fall, the management printed the usual call for townsfolk to turn out and see themselves on screen. *Moving Picture World* gave the movie only a passing review, but praised the St. Augustine location: "Many of the sets are quite beautiful, and the composition of many of the exteriors show an artist's touch." The plot involves a lovers' triangle in a Portuguese colony in Arabia. The wife of the chief justice is sent to seduce a young engineer and steal an incriminating letter. She refuses to surrender her virtue, but the engineer gives her the letter anyway because he has fallen in love with her. When a mob kills the chief justice, the wife is free to love the engineer. Tourneur received credit for his handling of the crowd scene.[28]

Petrova apparently shot at least a few scenes for yet another movie, *The Law of the Land*, in St. Augustine because when it appeared at the Jefferson the *St. Augustine Record* said "most of it was made right here" and that local people appear as "supers" in the film. Maurice Tourneur again directed and the two leading men from *Exile* also appear. The opening scene is set in a resort on the Riviera—the kind of locale St. Augustine often provided in films. Reviews of the movie praised its "exceptionally appropriate settings" without linking those settings to St. Augustine. The picture is based on a Broadway play that takes place for the most part indoors. The plot follows Petrova's character as she marries a cruel man to protect her mother from a scandal. When the husband abuses Petrova and her young son, she shoots and kills him. The drama of the play comes when the police try to determine who killed the man; when the detective realizes that it is the wife, he must decide whether or not the murder is justified. Petrova received praise for her ability to convey a range of emotions. "She exhibits many of the subtle half-disclosures of thought and feeling so essential in an interpretation of the up-to-date American woman."[29]

Brady/World

Among the various motion pictures being made in St. Augustine in January 1917 the film *Maternity* did not stand out as anything of special note. In fact, the company of players who came with Alice Brady seem to have spent only a brief time at the state School for the Deaf and Blind before returning to Jacksonville. The theme of the movie was a woman's dread of childbirth. Perhaps Brady's character had good reason to be afraid because in the movie's final scene the hospital catches fire, and the mother and child barely escape with their lives.[30]

Although her appearance in St. Augustine was fleeting, in the larger universe of the movie industry Alice Brady occupied an important place. Her father, William Brady, had started his career as both a producer of Broadway plays and a manager of professional boxers. He also pioneered in moviemaking and parleyed two of his interests into making the *Corbett-Fitzsimmons Fight* of 1897, the longest motion picture produced up to that time. In 1914 he formed the World Film Corporation to distribute motion pictures. He made his daughter Alice the star of a Brady production company. She would make many films, and successfully moved into talkies. In 1937 she won an Oscar as best supporting actress for *In Old Chicago*, but she is perhaps best remembered as the elderly mother of two brothers accused of murder who are defended by Henry Fonda in *Young Mr. Lincoln* (1939).

FAMOUS PLAYERS–LASKY CORPORATION

Marie Doro followed a familiar path on her way to becoming a movie star. She began as a chorus girl, graduated to playing minor parts on stage, and eventually made her way to Broadway where, among other roles, she acted opposite William Gillette in his landmark portrayal of Sherlock Holmes. While touring in Europe she appeared on stage with a teenaged Charlie Chaplin, who would later write that Marie Doro swept him off his feet—although she later confessed that she had no recollection of the youthful Chaplin. Doro's delicate beauty invited descriptions of her as a brunette Lillian Gish. By 1917 she had joined other noted stage actors as a member of the Famous Players ensemble.

In the film *Heart's Desire* St. Augustine does not appear in its usual guise as a tropical land, but is supposed to be the stark Breton coast of France. The company built peasant cottages for a fishing village on Anastasia Island and trimmed the fronds off of palm trees to disguise them. Many of the Famous Players crew traveled back and forth from Jacksonville daily, shooting Paris scenes indoors in the Jacksonville studio and outdoor views in St. Augustine. Doro escaped the rigors of commuting by rooming at the Buckingham Hotel and later the Alcazar. Eventually the moviemakers took over the Coquina Inn on Anastasia Island as a place where crew members could lodge and the company could store equipment. In addition to views taken at the prop village on the island, scenes were made at Whitney's Old House on Hospital Street, and the Catholic bishop was prevailed upon to stage a 250-person religious procession in front of the cameras. One night they took pictures in the dark on St. Francis Street. They also appeared on the grounds of Dr. Anderson's Markland, where a newsman reported, "a large crowd of spectators, as usual, forms an interested audience."[31]

One day, as Doro was riding in a car, people on the street recognized her and called out a request for a photo. "Without a moment's hesitation," reported the *St. Augustine Record*, she descended from her car and complied with the request, although the request was made by those who were utter strangers to her. They were delighted, and also a little surprised at the noted star's ready acquiescence."[32]

FOX FILM CORPORATION

St. Augustine's city leaders were continually on the lookout for opportunities to lure movie production companies to their city, and in early 1917 this vigilance paid off. City manager Winton L. Miller was riding one of Flagler's railway trains to Miami and happened to encounter Fox's Clifford P. Saum on the same train. Saum was on his way to Cuba in search of a sugarcane field to use as a setting for a Hawaiian movie. Miller assured him that he could find the required cane field near St. Augustine, and shortly thereafter the two men were scouting the country north of town for a cane field. When one was located, the movie man decided it was too far removed from town to be used conveniently, but Miller assured him that the cane stalks could be cut and replanted close to town.[33]

Thus on February 7 Miller and other town leaders stood on the platform at the railway station to welcome a forty-person crew of Fox personnel to the Ancient City. Leading the group was director J. Gordon Edwards, but the reception committee gave its greatest attention to the lead actress, Theda Bara, who in the words of one St. Augustinian, "really stood the town on its ear." She had previously made *A Fool There Was* and *The Devil's Daughter* in St. Augustine, and the *St. Augustine Record* declared her "the greatest screen vampire in the history of the silent drama." The two films Fox planned to make this time were however intended to cast Bara in "good woman" roles. The welcoming committee escorted Edwards, Bara, and some of the other leaders of the Fox party to the Hotel Alcazar, while the rest of the group found more modest accommodations. They were expected to stay for two months.[34]

Someone in town came up with the idea of holding a gala ceremony on the historic town plaza to commemorate the fact that Theda Bara's rapid rise to stardom had begun with the making of *A Fool There Was* in St. Augustine. Mayor James Ingraham, president of Henry Flagler's land company, set three o'clock on Saturday, February 17 as the moment of the great event, and long before that time the plaza thronged with curious spectators. The mayor drove to the Alcazar to pick up the guest of honor and then had a hard time pressing through the crowd with his famous visitor. The city band struck up a lively tune, and the police formed a wedge to deliver the mayor and his charge to the center of the plaza.

Mayor Ingraham made some brief remarks and presented Bara with a large bouquet of American Beauty roses. "Ladies and gentlemen," he concluded, "you will now see Miss Theda Bara in her great play of planting a Washingtonian palm in the Plaza of St. Augustine." Motion picture cameras recorded the event. Marguerite Capo, a local girl, later said, "I remember standing so near Theda Bara as she put a spade of dirt on the tree's roots that I was completely disillusioned. The mascara on and around her eyes was awful at close range." General J. Clifford R. Foster, commander of the Florida National Guard, finished with a little speech

Theda Bara received the applause of the citizens of St. Augustine when she planted a commemorative palm tree in the town's central plaza. Mayor James Ingraham
stands on her right. (Courtesy of P. K. Yonge Library of Florida History, University
of Florida)

and presented Bara with a copy of *The Unwritten History of Old St. Augustine*. The band struck up the *Star Spangled Banner* and Mayor Ingraham
escorted St. Augustine's adopted daughter back to the Hotel Alcazar.[35]
A month later Bara presented the city with a film recording of the tree-
planting ceremony. The Jefferson Theatre showed it for several evenings.[36]

Livingston Larned, the town's wintertime pundit, eulogized Fox's
troupe and their star attraction: "Mr. Fox's clever company of players,
camera men, scene painters and what nots hit the old town with all the
velocity of a tornado." He opined that Bara liked St. Augustine because it
possessed two big hotels and enough food for her and her maid. St. Augustine was not large enough to contain her, however. "Miss Bara belongs
to the world at large. She is a public institution. As the pet vampire of the
universe, she has no living peer."[37]

For *Heart and Soul* the Fox crew built a fort next to Evergreen Cemetery in West Augustine, then burned it down. (Courtesy of St. Augustine Historical Society)

Work on Bara's current production, *Her Greatest Love*, had already been started in the Fox studio in Fort Lee. For the exterior scenes St. Augustine provided the requisite European ambiance. The movie's big wedding scene was staged in the palm garden on the west lawn of the Hotel Ponce de Leon. Hundreds of the hotel's formally dressed patrons were invited to surround the bride and groom as the wedding audience. Among the guests playing parts was Chauncey Depew, former president of the New York Central Railroad and former U.S. senator. "With its distinctly foreign atmosphere, and old world charm of architecture and decoration, the Hotel Ponce de Leon makes a wonderful setting for a picture of this type," noted the *St. Augustine Record*. After shooting the scene, Bara was driven to Flagler Hospital to donate the floral decorations to patients in the hospital.[38]

When the film appeared at the Orpheum Theatre, the manager wrote, "Hundreds of home folks and thousands of visitors watched day by day the interesting work and the pretty scenes and it will be a real pleasure to see the results of Miss Bara's artistry on the screen." One of the local girls who watched the moviemakers was Clara M. Estes, and later she recalled that Bara wore large hats as she strolled in town and "had a slow sinuous walk." Estes added that Bara was "the first woman I ever saw who had her eyes so shadowed they looked almost black."[39]

Fox's next production was *Heart and Soul*, a story based on the popular Boer War novel *Jess* by Rider Haggard. The novel was set in South Africa, but Fox transferred the setting to Hawaii. Although alligators are not found in Hawaii, director Edwards could not resist putting one of Florida's most famous residents into the film. The crew visited the Alligator Farm on Anastasia Island; pulled out a big gator, said to be five hundred years old, from his comfortable pool; and placed him on a dirt road along which Bara was to ride. The gator refused to stay put for long, but ultimately, after much manhandling of the thrashing gator, the camera started to roll. Bara's horse shied at the sight of the gator and—according to Fox's publicity men—"Miss Bara flung herself clear of the horse, but tripped in the sand and fell only a few feet from the huge saurian. . . . Just as Miss Bara struggled to her feet he began to move his bulky form toward her, his mammoth jaws agape."[40]

An earlier newspaper story also bearing the mark of movie release hyperbole gave Bara high marks for managing to stay astride her horse. According to the account, Bara was riding down a street in town when an auto pulled out from a side street and caused her horse to rear and almost crash into a wall. "Miss Bara is a splendid horsewoman and demonstrated her ability to handle her high spirited animal by averting an accident, although the escape was a narrow one."[41]

Fox expended two weeks and a good deal of effort constructing the cane field, a military stockade, and a "South Sea Island home" on a large field in West St. Augustine. A number of palm trees and other shrubs were transplanted in the landscape. Some of the dry palmetto leaves were painted dark green so that they would show up more clearly on film. Livingston Larned came out, along with much of the year-round and transient population of the town, to watch the movie people at work. Boys sold cold drinks and peanuts to the spectators, and the crowd offered up running commentaries on the progress of the filmmaking. Larned described the movie lot as "sprinkled with autos, carriages, tourists on foot, babies in go-carts, bicycles, and, here and there, a luxurious closed car,

The Hawaiian plantation house in *Heart and Soul* was built with palm tree trunks as pillars. The fence around Evergreen Cemetery, which still stands, can be seen in the background. (Courtesy of St. Augustine Historical Society)

with a glimpse through the glass doors, of vivid green and orange sweaters, and a yawning bulldog and Miss Millionbucks, powdering her nose." Then at the proper moment Bara, "the Queen of the Vampires," "made up like a lime kiln, walks steadily up the path, oblivious to the eager eyes and the acenario [*sic*] difficulties of the much manhandled hero. The crowd barely manages to breathe." While others noted Bara's heavy eyeshadow, Larned commented on the white or yellow pancake makeup often used by actors so that their skin tones would appear natural on film.[42]

The grand climax of *Heart and Soul* was to be a great conflagration that would consume the sugarcane field and the "South Sea Island home," but the fire almost came off prematurely. A fire in the woods near the set brought the town's fire chief rushing out to the scene, but he determined that the fire was no threat to the movie company's props and, besides, the fire was outside the city limits. On March 28, the day before the Fox company planned to decamp for the North, the planned fire did sweep across the faux-Hawaiian landscape. Playing the role of revolutionaries, horsemen from the nearby farming communities of Hastings and Elkton swept down on the settlement with torches, setting fire to the place. Soon some of their fellow townsmen, acting as the U.S. cavalry, galloped up, with Bara riding at their head, to drive the rebels away. A large crowd of spectators cheered on the amateur actors.[43]

The movie magazine *Motography* gave the movie a good review: "There is excitement all through this, which as a melodrama with thrills and surface action is very passable. Daring horseback riding, thrilling rescues, violent scenes, villainous brutality and the like are all there." The story is of

Theda Bara did not wear elegant gowns in *Heart and Soul*. (From the author's collection)

a bandit rebel who wants to conquer the island and of two girls who love the same man. In the end Bara is the sister who summons the U.S. cavalry from their barracks (Fort Marion) and leads them to defeat the rebels. Bara received good marks for her "thoroughly artistic" death scene—which opened the way for her sister to get the hero. One reviewer wrote, "Admirers of Miss Bara will like this play immensely. Although the writer doesn't care for Miss Bara in 'goody-goody' roles, one must admit that she does some very clever work. Her riding is especially good." So perhaps Bara really was a good horsewoman. However, Kathryn Oliveros, who had stood in for Mary Keane in *The Hermit of Bird Island,* observed that for filming the most dangerous riding sequences the directors replaced Bara with an understudy.[44]

St. Augustine once again showed up well on screen. "The settings, mostly outdoors, and taken in a very beautiful section of the South, lend a great deal of charm to the picture." The hard work in building the sets and transplanting the cane field led to a highly dramatic fire scene.[45]

When the Orpheum Theatre showed the film, families from Hastings and Elkton drove to town in an "auto parade" to watch their menfolk perform on horseback. They packed the theater beyond standing room, while their parked cars and trucks encircled the plaza. As had become a regular feature of life in St. Augustine in recent years, viewers could recognize local places and familiar faces in the movie.[46]

During the filming of *Heart and Soul* Bara attempted to slip into the Orpheum Theatre without being recognized to see herself in *The Darling of Paris.* Although her companions tried to surround and shelter her, guests in the audience recognized St. Augustine's most famous adopted daughter and raised a fuss. Only when the houselights dimmed did she find the anonymity she desired. It was said that this was the first time she had ever visited a public theater to view herself on film.[47]

This episode in the winter of 1917 would be Bara's last visit to St. Augustine. Near the height of her fame at the time, she was Fox's biggest box office draw and most profitable property. In the summer of 1917 she and her family moved to California where she made *Cleopatra,* an epic motion picture best remembered for Bara's revealing Egyptian costumes. In 1919 she and Fox parted ways, perhaps because Fox chose not to pay

The best Bara picture ever made.
A great patriotic theme. Will thrill American audiences.
Get in touch with Fox Exchange Manager now and secure
your advertising allotment before the supply is exhausted.

Box Office Advice to Fox Exhibitors.
Use plenty of posters and newspaper stories.
HEART AND SOUL will be a great boost for
your theatre. Bill it strong and arrange for
a record breaking business.

Since World War I was being fought when *Heart and Soul* was released, the movie promoted patriotic fervor. (From *Moving Picture World*)

the enormous sums that Bara's celebrity earned her. She tried acting on Broadway and in a few other films, but she never regained her rank as a leading actress. Bara retired gracefully and lived a quiet life in southern California, largely forgotten by the public but still part of the circle of Hollywood figures living on the fringes of motion picture ballyhoo.

If anyone came close to rivaling Theda Bara as a star that St. Augustine could claim as its own, Johnny Ray and his wife, Emma, did. When they came to town in February 1917 it was something of a homecoming. The Rays had leased the Jefferson Theatre back in the fall of 1910 as a permanent home base for their vaudeville comedy act. For years they had been traveling the theater circuit portraying a lovable Irish couple (Johnny had actually been born in Wales). Although they called St. Augustine their new home, the Rays often took off during the years of their lease and traveled the country, leaving Harry P. Davis to manage the Jefferson.[48]

In 1916 the Rays organized the Reserve Photoplays Company in their northern hometown of Cleveland and went into the moviemaking business. They produced a set of "Casey" comedy shorts with Johnny as a "harmless, loveable Irish laborer" and Emma as his affectionate wife. The Rays employed amateurs to fill out the casts of their plays. When the Rays showed their efforts to motion picture distributors, the reviewers felt there was "nothing new" in the films, just standard vaudeville slapstick comedy: Casey dreams he is rich and hobnobs with the "swells," Casey directs a band, Casey is a fireman, and such.[49]

In February 1917 the Rays met with the St. Augustine Chamber of Commerce, seeking a studio location where they could produce films. They said that they wanted to make two-reel comedies, starting small and building up the business. In the end, the Rays leased space in the new studio in Jacksonville recently erected by the noted architect Henry Klutho. (It was indicative of the decline of moviemaking in Jacksonville that the Rays were the only tenants to rent space in Klutho's studio.) In early March the Rays were back in town, saying that they expected to return in the fall to build a studio of their own in St. Augustine. In the meantime they put out the word that they needed a small dog and several young men and women to play roles in their new film *Coughing Higgins*. Each day bunches of spectators gathered on Central Avenue, San Marco Avenue, and around a hot dog stand in the plaza to watch the Rays enact their cinema drama. Late in March the Rays departed from town, saying that they hoped to return in the fall. Johnny warned that if St. Augustine ever hoped to attract motion picture companies on a more permanent basis, it would

Johnny and Emma Ray were an old vaudeville team that made some short motion picture comedies but never quite hit it big. (From *Moving Picture World*)

have to provide properly equipped studios—but the failure of the Klutho studio in Jacksonville to attract clients showed the risk of constructing a studio in the hope of attracting customers, and St. Augustine never chose that path.[50]

That summer the General Film Company began releasing all the Johnny Ray films, including the previously made Casey shorts, new "Muggy" comedies, and *Coughing Higgins*. The company took out a full-page ad in *Moving Picture World* promoting the Ray productions. Evidently not many theaters wanted the films. *Coughing Higgins* was shown at the Orpheum in October, and after that the Ray productions disappeared from the pages of the motion picture trade journals and popular magazines.[51]

Johnny Ray came back in 1920 as "Jiggs," the father in the popular newspaper comic strip "Bringing Up Father" by George McManus. Unfortunately, the comic strip characters did not translate well to the screen and only three *Bringing Up Father* two-reel comedies were made. Ray died in 1927, but his widow, Emma, continued to appear in small parts in films at least until 1933. She passed away in 1935.[52]

IVAN FILM COMPANY

In late March Ivan Abramson, owner and director of Ivan Film Company, brought a party of actors to stay at the Hotel Alcazar for just four or five days. He had come to find sunshine and warm air—not tropical scenery—in order to complete a few scenes in his gigantic eight-reel film *One Law for Both*. Abramson was noted for making "problem plays" that dramatized social issues. This film tackles two issues: the double standard for the sexual behavior of men and women, and the double standard under law for Russian aristocrats and peasants. Both issues were being strenuously debated at the time. The film switched back and forth from America to Russia (confusing movie audiences). In America the proper role of the "new woman" had already entered the popular imagination—years before the "Roaring Twenties"—while in Russia the turmoil that would lead to the Bolshevik Revolution in December had already broken into violent clashes between mobs and the tsar's soldiers.[53]

In the spring of 1917 St. Augustine played a small part in what continues to be a motion picture mystery. Earlier in the year Edwin August, a veteran filmmaker who had started with Edison in 1908, came to Jacksonville with the announced plan of making "natural color" movies at a studio he would establish there. Supposedly he had good financial backing for his enterprise, and he was said to be perfecting a process for making films in color. Up to that time only a few commercial films had been laboriously hand-tinted, and a few movies had been made in Europe and the United States with various experimental processes that produced color. *Variety* magazine published a story saying that August had already finished eight reels of film for a movie to be called *A Tale of Two Nations.*[54]

On May 17 the *St. Augustine Record* ran a want ad for "15 young men and 12 young women for moving picture to be staged in and around St. Augustine." The prospective "supers" were to apply at the Monson Hotel, where August and a dozen of his crew were lodging. The *Record* said, "St. Augustine scenes and some of our old historical relics will serve as a unique setting and import 'atmosphere' of an unusual sort to the picture." A few days later the players were reported to have been working in the Garnett orange grove.[55]

After that, nothing more was ever published about August's company or his prospective "natural color" motion picture in any of the motion picture trade magazines, although August continued to play minor parts in movies for more than another decade.

FAMOUS PLAYERS–LASKY CORPORATION

Summer was well advanced when a small crew of performers from the Famous Players company came to St. Augustine to spend just four days shooting some specific scenes for *Barbary Sheep*. Maurice Tourneur, who had worked with Petrova just weeks earlier, was responsible for the film. Actress Elsie Ferguson, who reportedly brought two maids with her, plays a wife who is abandoned in an Algerian hotel while her husband, oblivious to the danger of leaving his spouse unattended, treks into the mountains hunting mountain sheep. Left to her own imagination in an exotic

Elsie Ferguson and her movie husband, Lumsden Hare, stand near the steps to one of the ladies' entrances to the Hotel Ponce de Leon—a frequently used setting in films requiring an intriguing aspect. (Courtesy of New York Public Library)

location, she almost succumbs to the romantic advances of a French-speaking Bedouin, played by Pedro de Cordoba (who actually had been born in New York City).

Tourneur's re-creation of North Africa was noted by reviewers for its dramatic scenery: "the settings are masterpieces of pictorial beauty. . . . It is a remarkable thing that the same sets, no matter how massive, are not, or at least do not have the appearance of being used twice." A large set was built along a street in Fort Lee, New Jersey, for a sweeping street scene, and the Algerian mountain scenes must surely have been taken in the Hudson River Palisades. St. Augustine, however, supplied desert vistas from Anastasia Island's sand dunes, one of the ladies' entrances to the Hotel Ponce de Leon served as the entrance to the Algerian hotel, and some footage was taken at the old Espinosa-Pérez-Sánchez House, which stood just across Treasury Street from the Monson Hotel where the movie company stayed.[56]

St. Augustine could put 1917 into the books as another successful moviemaking year, but now the long-expected U.S. entry into the war had arrived, and its impact on all aspects of life could not be predicted.

A pair of freshly poured concrete posts provide rustic props for Elsie Ferguson in a desert scene from *Barbary Sheep*. The location is Anastasia Island, not North Africa. (Courtesy of New York Public Library)

7

WARTIME CONDITIONS

1917–1918

In October 1917 renowned opera diva Mary Garden took what she called a "flying trip" to St. Augustine to shoot some "desert" scenes for the movie version of the opera *Thais* in which she had gained celebrity. City manager W. L. Miller and the chairman of the Chamber of ommerce were at the railway station to greet the first of what they expected to be several film companies to visit that winter season.

The Goldwyn Pictures company checked in at the Monson Hotel, but director Frank Crane and Miller left immediately by car for a trip across the Matanzas Bay bridge and down to the beach to find likely spots for desert scenes. Garden, her sister, and some of the rest of the crew walked to Fort Marion to see the old stone fortification. The St. Augustine Historical Society, which gave tours of the site, received a generous donation from Garden.

The next morning the cast and crew made the trip over the bridge and to the ocean by auto and gathered on the beach—except for Margaret Townsend, whose flivver had taken a wrong turn down a stretch of sandy road and gotten lost. A quick search by the movie people located her. Thanks to bright sunshine, the cameramen finished shooting in just a few hours. Garden complained that working in the Florida sun was harder on her eyes than working under Klieg lights in a studio. After just four days the Goldwyn folks were on the train back to the Fort Lee studio.[1]

The story of *Thais* is that of a wicked woman in early Christian-era Alexandria, Egypt, who is led by a holy man to journey across a desert to a nunnery in order to save her soul. Along the way, however, the holy man falls in love with the wicked woman, complicating the plot. Garden is the center of attention in the movie—especially when dressed in a revealing "flimsy chiffon robe." Garden was a full-bodied, forty-three-year-old opera singer, not one of the slender young females favored by moviemakers at the time, yet she had a reputation as a stalwart of feminine beauty. The reviewer for *Motion Picture News* praised the "magnificent staging" of the film, including the desert scenes. "The gowns worn by Miss Garden are little short of wonderful. . . . At another time Miss Garden appears in the desert in a diaphanous garb that reveals every line of her form." Another reviewer was less enthusiastic: "Miss Garden's acting, however, is the weak feature of the play. She evidently is camera-conscious and she poses rather than acts."[2]

METRO/COLUMBIA PICTURES CORPORATION

In early December Alla Nazimova, a Russian-born star of the live stage, arrived at the Hotel Alcazar with about twenty other players and technicians from the Metro company to make "a gypsy picture." Nazimova had just worked on *The Revelation*, the exterior scenes of which had been filmed in New Orleans in order to capture Old World streetscapes. When *The Revelation* was screened at the Jefferson months later, the management claimed that it had been "partly" made in St. Augustine; so evidently while in St. Augustine Metro took some additional "European" scenes to finish the film.[3]

However, the company's main mission in Florida was to complete a big seven-reel drama entitled *Toys of Fate*. The director was George D. Baker, who had directed Emmy Wehlen in *Duchess of Doubt* the previous season. Nazimova plays both mother and daughter roles. First, she is the wife of a gypsy chief who deserts him to live with the wealthy owner of a vast estate where the wandering gypsies sometimes camp. When the rich man tires of the gypsy woman, she commits suicide. Years later the gypsy band returns to the estate, and Nazimova plays the role of the daughter, who likewise becomes involved with the rich man but really loves the

The west lawn of the Hotel Ponce de Leon was the location for this scene from *Toys of Fate*. Charles Bryant approaches Alla Nazimova. (From *Moving Picture World*)

rich man's lawyer. Overlapping lovers' triangles lead to strife and murder, but ultimately Nazimova and the lawyer are united. Some of the scenes for *Toys of Fate* were shot on the grounds of the Hotel Ponce de Leon, and a movie magazine says that the gypsies' camp was at "Ponce de Leon Springs," which must be Fountain of Youth Park where Pathé had located its outdoor studio and menagerie back in 1914. *Motion Picture News* liked the film, saying, "Most of the scenes have been taken outdoors and are very beautiful."[4]

FAMOUS PLAYERS–LASKY CORPORATION

During the winter of 1917–1918 very few movie people came down to Jacksonville to inhabit the studios. The Famous Players were the exception. Pauline Frederick led the acting contingent. She had made *Bella Donna* in St. Augustine in 1915, and *The Spider* in 1916, and now she was back in Florida again. In early November 1917, director Robert G. Vignola brought a

The summer day is forgotten, while Azah learns her alphabet.

NAZIMOVA
TOYS OF FATE

In *Toys of Fate* Alla Nazimova and Irving Cummings share a moment under the spreading live oak trees at what is today Fountain of Youth Archaeological Park. The ancient oaks in the park continue to provide one of the most scenic locations in St. Augustine. (From the author's collection)

small number of players from Jacksonville to St. Augustine to shoot some scenes for *Madame Jealousy*, an allegorical drama of human emotions, virtues, and vices based on a play by George V. Hobart. Frederick filled the title role as Madame Jealousy, while handsome Thomas Meighan enacted Valor. Some of the other characters represented Pride, Finance, Charm, and the like. In a story of two families in conflict, Happiness (a baby) wins in the end.[5]

Pauline Frederick and Jules Raucourt enjoy a quiet moment on the loggia of the Hotel Ponce de Leon. (Courtesy of Greta de Groat)

The company's larger project was transforming the opera *La Tosca* into a motion picture. Edward José, a familiar face in St. Augustine from *Perils of Pauline* and *A Fool There Was*, directed the production. Frederick and some of the company boarded at the Monson Hotel, just down the bay front from Fort Marion, where work on the film began. Some continued to live in Jacksonville and make the thirty-five-mile commute over the recently constructed brick road. To hold down costs the road had been made only nine feet wide. When cars met coming in opposite directions, each had to steer two wheels off the side of the road to make room to pass.

One day a party of moviemakers turned their auto into the deep sand beside the road and flipped the vehicle. No one was badly hurt, but the car was banged up. On a brighter note, Frederick, her mother, and Frank Losee (the villain in *La Tosca*) attended an afternoon showing of *Bab's Matinee Idol* in which Losee played a part.[6]

Fort Marion served as the stage for many of the scenes in the movie. Many local residents and winter visitors turned out to watch the action. An execution by hanging received a "very realistic" endorsement from one spectator. Margaret Capo, a local youngster, was sent to bring home

In this photo from *La Tosca* Jules Raucourt and Pauline Frederick stand at the door to the rebuilt chapel inside Fort Marion. (Courtesy of Greta de Groat)

her five-year-old brother and found him sitting in Pauline Frederick's lap. A firing squad scene figured prominently in the screenplay, and the movie crew built a wooden wall in front of one of the stone walls of the fort where the condemned man would stand. The correspondent for *Moving Picture World* explained, "At Fort Marion the wall that was used for executions of this kind still stands, and the jagged bullet holes are mute evidence of the tragedies that have been enacted in the past." (There are indeed pockmarks in the wall of the northeast bastion of the fort today, but certainly not as a result of firing squads.)[7]

After shooting some scenes at the Hotel Ponce de Leon, the Famous Players departed on December 13 having spent just ten days in St. Augustine. The film was finished at the company's studio on Fifty-Sixth Street in New York. Frederick reportedly went home with a head cold "due to the fact that Miss Frederick was playing Tosca, another famous lady who never acquired the habit of dressing for the rigors of winter time."[8]

PETROVA PICTURE COMPANY–FIRST NATIONAL

Mademoiselle Olga Petrova came back to St. Augustine in December 1917 at the head of a movie company bearing her name. In the spring she and Jesse Lasky had parted ways—reluctantly, according to Petrova. Her new backers were Frederick L. Collins, editor of *McClure's Magazine*, and a band of theater owners who objected to "block booking," which required them to take all the movies offered by a distribution company, even if they wanted to select only some of the offerings. Their company, First National, rented a studio in New York City to shoot interior scenes for the new movie, but most of the exteriors were made in St. Augustine.[9]

Daughter of Destiny had been written by Petrova as a vehicle to display the virtues of a strong woman. In Petrova's opinion it was "the most pretentious production I had yet been associated with." Brought out during World War I, the story tells of the daughter of an American ambassador who marries the crown prince of a fictitious European kingdom. When the secret agent of another country stirs up a rebellion, Petrova's character ("a stately and finely gowned figure," according to a review) courageously supports her husband in suppressing the uprising. The moral was that American women should support their men in the war against Germany.

When the movie appeared at the Jefferson Theatre, women in the audience received photographs of Petrova.[10]

Unfortunately for Petrova's motion picture career, First National suffered from a lack of its own theater outlets and, allegedly, from a "lockout" by other distributors who refused to handle their films. Following an exhausting nationwide tour to sell war bonds, Petrova retired from the movies. She and her husband purchased a large estate on Long Island that provided her with a peaceful home base. Soon she returned to the live stage, writing two plays in which she starred on cross-country tours. In 1977 she passed away in Clearwater, Florida.[11]

THE JEFFERSON AND ORPHEUM THEATRES

The American entry into World War I impacted local movie theaters across the nation. The most immediate and visible effect of the war was an increase in the price of admission. To help finance the war Congress enacted new taxes on tobacco products, train fares, telegraph messages, and theater admission tickets. Movie companies were also taxed on each foot of film released. In St. Augustine that meant a one-cent tax on a ten-cent ticket, two cents on a fifteen-cent ticket, and three cents on a thirty-cent ticket. Moviegoers were advised to "take pennies to the movies."[12]

A more serious situation developed as cold winter weather set in. The Federal Fuel Administration allocated large amounts of coal for use by the Army and Navy, leaving civilian consumers with shortages. Northern states, where household and business heating were deemed more crucial, received a greater allotment of coal than southern states. In St. Augustine the city government established a program to purchase firewood from rural landowners in the area and haul it to a vacant lot in town where citizens could purchase wood for heating and cooking.[13]

To conserve coal the national fuel administrator ordered "Heatless Mondays," when all places of business were ordered to shut down their furnaces and turn off their electric lights. Theater owners managed to get an exemption, allowing them to stay open on Mondays so that employees of closed businesses could at least go to the movies. The theaters' day to close would be Tuesday. After just three weeks—late January to early February—the heatless days were suspended in the southern states, and later in February the order was suspended for the whole nation. The government apparently decided that the heatless, lightless days saved little fuel and caused too much disruption to normal business. One movie magazine, however, observed that the experience did remind people that there was a war going on.[14]

The war may have had an impact on movie production as well. Companies made fewer films in the months just before and after the declaration of war because they were not sure what effect it would have on society and the economy. Overall, 8,436 films were released in 1917, compared to 9,180 in 1916, an 8 percent decrease. However, the decline in numbers may have had little significance since most of the falloff came in one-reel shorts.[15]

The early years of the twentieth century marked the high tide of racial segregation, by custom and by law, in the United States. Although motion pictures represented an almost all-white art form, black Americans were just as fascinated by the movies as whites were. Usually black patrons found admission to theaters, but they were restricted to seating in one specific area, often in the balcony. In St. Augustine there had been attempts to operate a theater for black patrons on Washington Street, the business street of Lincolnville, the town's black neighborhood. In the summer of 1918 this theater closed, probably for business reasons, since the summer months were slow. The Jefferson announced that the "entire gallery" (apparently as opposed to just a section of the gallery) of the theater would now be reserved for black patrons. They could buy tickets and enter the theater from a side door on Cordova Street that led directly to the balcony. On the first night of this new policy about one hundred black movie fans attended.[16]

Frank Genovar of the Orpheum leased the closed black theater in Lincolnville and announced its reopening, with showings on Tuesday, Thursday, and Saturday evenings. It is doubtful that the theater was able to survive long. No further notices of this theater appear in the newspaper.[17]

FAMOUS PLAYERS–LASKY CORPORATION

Another Famous Players company arrived in St. Augustine in early February, but they came up from Miami, not down from New York. Florenz Ziegfeld and his wife, Billie Burke, headed the small group. As one of the

In the farce *Let's Get a Divorce*, Billie Burke (Mrs. Florenz Ziegfeld) plays a girl who grew up living a sheltered life and longs for the excitement of romance. (Courtesy of George Eastman Museum)

most illustrious couples in the country, the Ziegfelds naturally took a room at the elegant Hotel Ponce de Leon. Ziegfeld was famous for his follies, which brought some of the most talented performers and glamorous showgirls to his stage. His wife had become one of the most popular actresses in films, mainly in high-society dramas and rollicking comedies. On the afternoon of their arrival Mr. Ziegfeld led a walk around town in search of the Catholic convent and lush gardens needed for the film *Let's Get a Divorce*. The moviemakers found their convent in the Sisters of St. Joseph's large house and school, and the town abounded with gardens grand and small. Later reviews said, "Beautiful backgrounds were secured in Florida."[18]

In *Let's Get a Divorce* Burke is a young woman raised in a sheltered convent who marries a wealthy but dreary middle-aged author. She yearns for the excitement of romance, and an intriguing illicit affair happens to present itself in the form of the husband's willing cousin. The astute husband detects the possibility of a dangerous liaison and decides to call his wife's bluff. He offers his wife a divorce and his cousin a large cash settlement for taking his wife off his hands. However, once the wife realizes that she can actually have the cousin, with no secrets or clandestine meetings, the intrigue disappears from the relationship, and she realizes that the cousin is going to turn into just another "husband." The husband plans one last encounter, allowing the cousin to reveal his shallow nature, and the wife decides that a good husband is better than romantic fantasies.

Ziegfeld, a supreme showman himself, enjoyed watching the actors cavort before the camera. Scattered showers threatened the players on occasion, but most of the time the sun provided just the help needed to complete the scenes. Burke exhibited the slightly off-center vivaciousness that would later make her popular in daffy older-matron roles in talking movies and shows up a little in her portrayal of Glinda the Good Witch in *The Wizard of Oz.*[19]

While the interior scenes of *Let's Get a Divorce* were being completed in New York, director Joseph Kaufman died of "pneumonia" supposedly contracted while he was in Florida. He was only thirty-five years old. Kaufman may actually have been an early victim of the "Spanish flu" that would take the lives of millions of mostly young people around the world. St. Augustine would have been a likely place to contract influenza, since it received thousands of visitors each winter and soldiers stationed in nearby Jacksonville were among those coming to town.[20]

WORLD FILM COMPANY

As the winter season of 1918 began to wind down, one more movie company paid a visit to St. Augustine. The World Film Company sent director Travers Vale to Florida to film an "Oriental" movie. Vale and his wife,

Louise, made the Monson Hotel on the bayfront their headquarters, while the rest of the company went to the Hotel Alcazar, a livelier spot more entertaining for younger folks. Vale told a local newspaperman that he liked the exotic atmosphere of St. Augustine. He added that wartime restrictions on travel would direct more moviemakers to Florida because it was closer than California to northeastern motion picture offices.[21]

Since their film, *Vengeance*, required settings in both England and India, the players traveled to various parts of town to find likely locations. The company's carpenters built an Indian bungalow on the lawn of Fort Marion. One reviewer of the completed film declared that the movie was "lavishly produced and is possessed of a realistic atmosphere of far-eastern India when the action shifts from England." The English-born Montagu Love plays two roles in the picture, father and son. The story involves an English gentleman who takes the blame for his brother's cheating at cards and goes into exile in India. Years later the gentleman's son, born of an Indian mother, returns to England. During the filming Love became "quite ill" and was checked into the local hospital. Perhaps he also was a victim of the flu.[22]

The youngest actor in the film, Madge Evans, would go on to enjoy a full career in motion pictures. Although she was only nine years old at the time of *Vengeance*, she had already been acting for several years—and she would grow up to play wholesome "all-American girl" roles throughout the 1930s.

The return of cool weather in the fall of 1918 brought another, much more devastating wave of influenza to the world. In St. Augustine schools and churches were closed, and all public gatherings were banned. Both the Jefferson and Orpheum theaters closed on October 6 and did not reopen until November 2. When the re-openings were announced, the managers advertised that the Jefferson had been "thoroughly fumigated" and the Orpheum "cleaned, disinfected, repainted." Patrons attending a show at the Jefferson just after its reopening got a scare of a different sort when a fire broke out in the projection booth and everyone flooded out of the exits. The nitrate film had broken in the projector and caught fire, a not uncommon occurrence with the primitive equipment of the day, but this small fire ignited two rolls of film that had been left out ready for reel changes. The projectionist and manager quickly smothered the flames, but the projectionist suffered severe burns. The next night the theater opened as usual.[23]

St. Augustine's theaters were caught up in another sweeping development at the same time as the influenza epidemic. Stephen A. Lynch, owner of a chain of theaters in the South, purchased both the Jefferson and the Orpheum. Lynch was part of Paramount's attempt to dominate motion picture distribution in America. They led in "block bookings," demanding that independent theaters take all the films Paramount offered in order to get any of the popular Famous Player–Lasky films, especially those starring "America's Sweetheart," Mary Pickford. The merger of the Jefferson and Orpheum under one management was part of a major consolidation movement in the film industry. As in so many American industries, the days of many small companies were giving way to an era dominated by a few large companies.[24]

8

INTO THE SUNSET

1919 TO "THE END"

The new year, 1919, opened with high hopes in St. Augustine for a return to normalcy in winter moviemaking following the conclusion of World War I. Only seven films had been made in town in 1918, compared to nineteen the year before.

In early January a *St. Augustine Record* headline announced, "Motion Picture Folk Beginning to Arrive." The article said that a company of players from the World Film Company would soon be coming to town to produce a major motion picture. The paper ran an editorial repeating the now-familiar arguments for why Florida was superior to California as a location for film companies. It added, "There are scenes for certain types of pictures that can be filmed only in St. Augustine, owing to the fact that the old streets, quaint buildings and magnificent hotels of distinctly foreign architecture offer settings that are rare indeed." As it turned out, these high hopes would not be fulfilled. No other companies followed World Film, and only one motion picture would be made in town in 1919.[1]

The landscape of the motion picture industry had changed dramatically in the five years since 1914. Fewer movies were being made with each passing year, and those that were made ran to five reels or more. The day of one-reel shorts was just about gone, except for comedies. No longer could Thanhouser boast of releasing two movies a week. In fact, Thanhouser no longer existed. Edwin Thanhouser had not been able to change with the times, and he refused to move to southern California as so many of his contemporaries were doing. So Thanhouser disappeared. Other companies that had made films in St. Augustine likewise were gone: Kalem, Lubin, Selig, Comet, Reliance, Stellar, Equitable, and Vim. Edison, Aetna, and Gaumont were fast fading from the scene. Pathé concentrated on making comedy shorts and weekly newsreels. The venerable Vitagraph company was wobbling on its last legs and would be absorbed by newcomer Warner Brothers in 1925.

In Jacksonville, which boasted that a thousand movies had been made there, only two or three companies making comedy shorts pretended to maintain a presence. The newly built Thanhouser and Klutho studios advertised for companies to come and utilize their vacant facilities, but soon these ads disappeared from the trade journals. The Jacksonville Chamber of Commerce extended the usual invitation for moviemakers to "get out of the slush, ice and pneumonia" by coming to sunny Florida, but that effort paid no dividends. In 1921 the Jacksonville business community made one last grand effort by offering to turn the Army's abandoned Fort Johnston into "Fine Arts City," but no northern film companies took them up on the offer.[2]

Although a number of smaller companies still maintained studios in the East, and industry giant Paramount would build a new studio in New York City in 1920, the epicenter of motion picture production had settled in Southern California where warm weather and clear skies prevailed year-round. Florida moviemaking had always been limited to the winter months, and that seasonal limitation did not invite the establishment of permanent studios in the state. Florida had been an adjunct to New York, and when the companies went west, Florida lost out.

WORLD FILM COMPANY

Nevertheless, in January 1919 when World Film's cast and crew checked in to the Hotel Alcazar, St. Augustine seemed to have maintained its position as a pleasant location for wintertime moviemaking. June Elvidge, Carlyle Blackwell, Montagu Love, and a half dozen others performed in front of the camera at various locations in town for the movie *Three Green Eyes*. Elvidge and Blackwell play the roles of young romantics, while Love

Carlyle Blackwell and June Elvidge meet at the balcony of the often-photographed home of William A. Knight in a scene from *Three Green Eyes*. (From *Picture Play Magazine*)

serves as the wealthy businessman whom Elvidge is obliged to marry. (Love had played a similarly dignified role in the previous year's film *Vengeance*.) During the filming Elvidge took the opportunity to attend an evening showing at the Orpheum of *The Zero Hour*, a movie in which she had previously starred. In *Three Green Eyes* Elvidge comes to love her husband and attempts to recover a compromising letter she had written to Blackwell on the day before her marriage. A series of comic episodes ensues in pursuit of the letter, and meanwhile Blackwell finds a new love.[3]

COSMOPOLITAN

More than a year would pass before another motion picture company would come calling at St. Augustine. Three veterans of former forays into town led the way. Robert G. Vignola (*The Spider, Don Caesar de Bazan, Madame Jealousy*) was the director, while Montagu Love (*Vengeance, Three Green Eyes*) played the leading role of Don Julian, and Pedro de Cordoba (*One Law for Both, Barbary Sheep*) filled a minor role. All were now working for Cosmopolitan, a Paramount production company. The party of seventeen arrived in the midst of a week of rainy weather that climaxed with a tempest of wind and deluge of rain that flooded the streets around the Hotel Alcazar where they stayed. Outside town in the fields and pine flatwoods water stood a foot deep. Both railroad and automobile traffic was halted by washouts. Director Vignola quipped that he was being given a splendid opportunity to secure water scenes and flood pictures without making a special trip to Venice.[4]

Marooned in the Alcazar with the other hotel guests, the actors made the best of the situation and staged an impromptu entertainment. Montagu Love performed a pantomime; Gaston Glass, a Parisian, recited in French several poems made famous by Sarah Bernhardt; Philip Carle recited "The Cremation of Sam McGee"; and Vignola rendered "Napoleon's Last Farewell to His Troops."[5]

When the sun returned, the actors performed for the camera at Fort Marion, the Villa Zorayda, and Memorial Presbyterian Church. A large number of local people filled a crowd scene at the fort, and some locally prominent ladies dressed as Spanish matrons for an episode at the church. Groups of tourists and local citizens stood by as spectators. Cosmopolitan also constructed a large and elaborate set in its downtown New York studio. Their production was *The World and His Wife*, a film version of a successful stage play. Love played the husband and Alma Rubens the wife. So far as the reviewer for *Motion Picture News* was concerned, this tale of lives ruined by gossip in modern-day Spain was more notable for its backgrounds and settings than for its overly "psychological" story.[6]

Rubens, the female lead in the movie, enjoyed a spectacular career that was cut short by her addiction to heroin. She would die in 1931 at the age of just thirty-four. However, her colleagues enjoyed long careers. Director Vignola made many silent films and a few sound features during the 1930s before retiring. Love was already a major star in the motion picture firmament, and he would continue a noted career on Broadway and in motion pictures all the way through the 1930s. Standing over six feet tall and with a leonine head, Love was usually cast as a dignified figure of one sort or another, although he played the villain opposite Rudolph Valentino in *The Son of the Sheik* and dueled with John Barrymore in *Don Juan*. Pedro de Cordoba became one of Hollywood's most reliable character actors, playing supporting roles in dozens of major films until the year 1951. He even appeared in two episodes of *The Lone Ranger* television series.

FROHMAN

In late April 1920 a crew from the Frohman Amusement Corporation stopped by St. Augustine and worked just one day to take some shots for the fifteen-episode serial *The Invisible Ray*. They had been as far west as Los Angeles and as far south as Miami, shooting various scenes for their action-and-thrills adventure. The complicated plot revolves around a powerful ray with destructive force that can be used for evil if a gang of outlaws gets their hands on it. Ruth Clifford and Jack Sherrill star in this typical serial that depends on stunts such as jumping from one moving car to another, dropping from an airplane, and other daredevil acts. The most significant feature of this series is that it featured Ruth Clifford, who would live to be almost ninety-nine years old and would play roles as leading lady in silent films, supporting actress in talkies, and character actor in movies and television down to the year 1977, when she appeared on the television series *Police Story*.[7]

On April 26, 1920, a small contingent of actors, their families, and a technical crew arrived on the morning train and checked in to the modest St. George Hotel on St. George Street. This late in the season all the grand hotels had already closed. The most familiar face in the group was Alex

Director James Vincent and Rudolph Valentino start a carriage tour of St. Augustine's sites while filming *Stolen Moments*. This photo was taken from the front yard of the St. George Hotel on South St. George Street where the company stayed. Across the street is the office of Dr. Horace Lindsley. The small building housing his office has been torn down, but the colonial Horruytiner house on the right still remains as a historic landmark. (Courtesy of Joseph Yranski)

Alex Shannon, Aileen Pringle, and Rudolph Valentino stand in the garden courtyard of the Hotel Ponce de Leon. (Courtesy of Margaret Herrick Museum)

Shannon, a veteran thespian who had visited St. Augustine many times with traveling troupes and in the mid-1880s had briefly been co-manager of Genovar's Opera House. In 1917 he had played a supporting role in *Barbary Sheep*. Also notable in the company was George Bunny, son of John Bunny, the most popular comic actor of early silent films who had passed away shortly before. Marguerite Namara was the most famous of the party, having gained notoriety as a singer on Broadway and in grand opera—she had succeeded Mary Garden in *Thais*. Since the company had come to shoot "Brazilian" exterior scenes, an exotic-looking actor the *St. Augustine Record* identified as "Rudolfo" Valentino filled out the cast.[8]

The American Cinema Company ensemble wasted no time in getting down to business filming *Stolen Moments*. The afternoon of their arrival found them at the Hotel Ponce de Leon shooting scenes in the gardens and courtyard. A crowd of onlookers watched the action. The crew then moved on to Fort Marion and the Villa Zorayda to collect more scenery. After just four days they boarded a train for the north, saying that they had

The company from *Stolen Moments* strike theatrical poses for the camera. Director James Vincent shouts at Rudolph Valentino (with his arms raised), while Jean Gauthier and Aileen Pringle plead with him. An often-photographed ladies' entrance to the Hotel Ponce de Leon is in the background. (Courtesy of Joseph Yranski)

enjoyed their stay and hoped to return again. They would take some more footage in Savannah on their way home.[9]

The man the *Record* identified as "Rudolfo" was, of course, Rudolph (born Rodolfo) Valentino, who had broken into the movies only recently, playing minor roles, often as a villain because of his foreign looks. Born in Italy, he came to New York as an eighteen-year-old in 1913. He found a niche in the entertainment business as a suave Latin dancer exhibiting the latest dance steps at afternoon tea dances during the tango craze that swept the country before World War I. He achieved a degree of fame as partner to Joan Sawyer and even performed before President Wilson in Washington. Valentino then abandoned a touring theater company in

California and went to Los Angeles, where he hoped to make a career as a movie actor. His secondary role as a deceitful foreigner in *Stolen Moments* typified the kind of part he was given at the time. This would be the last time he played the role of a villain.

The film premiered in December 1920 without much fanfare, but when Rudolph Valentino became famous for his role in *The Four Horsemen of the Apocalypse* just a year later, the movie was re-released. Unfortunately, it was cut from six reels to just three, and only the shorter version has survived today. In this version there are no scenes of Fort Marion or the Zorayda, but the Hotel Ponce de Leon's courtyard is easily recognizable.

In the story Namara plays a writer with a home in Savannah who is in love with Valentino's character, Jose Dalmarez, a Brazilian novelist. He tries to entice her to come with him to Brazil but admits that he does not have marriage in mind. Namara refuses and later marries another man. Meanwhile, Valentino returns to Brazil and attempts to seduce Aileen Pringle, daughter of a Brazilian government official (played by Alex Shannon). Pringle's brother, portrayed by Jean Gauthier, tries to protect the virtue of his sister and engages in an athletic fistfight with Valentino in the courtyard of the Ponce de Leon. Valentino returns to Savannah and attempts to blackmail Namara with a love letter she had written to him before her marriage. When Valentino is subsequently murdered, suspicion falls on Namara, whose life hangs in the balance until a plot twist at the end reveals the true murderer.

Although his role in *Stolen Moments* was too small to advance Valentino's reputation, his subsequent films, especially *The Sheik*, would launch him to stardom as the matinee idol that women hoped would abduct them to his harem in the desert and that men wished they could emulate. Then in 1926 he died unexpectedly after surgery on severe gastric ulcers led to a massive internal infection. The emotional outpouring of grief across the United States testified to the grip moving picture stars held on popular imagination.

VITAGRAPH

A little more than a week after the American Cinema party left, a group from the old Vitagraph Company arrived at the Marion Hotel. George L.

Sargent, the director, had already been in town for two days searching for locations. Their motion picture, *The Whisper Market* (1920), was set in some unnamed South American city, and thus the usual "Spanish" locations around town were used as settings: the grounds of the Hotel Ponce de Leon, the garden of the Villa Flora, and narrow Green Street (soon to be renamed Cadiz Street). Since the scenario involved a women's dress shop, Deardorff's shop in the Hotel Cordova building on King Street served as the location for one scene. This shooting happened to take place on a Thursday afternoon when, by custom, the town took a half-holiday, and a larger than usual crowd of onlookers gathered to watch. A well-known landau carriage owned by the local transfer company also played a part in the story.[10]

Corinne Griffith stars in the movie as the wife of the American consul in a country presumed to be Brazil. She is the center of social life among the foreign colony in town and even is part owner of a women's dress shop. This, of course, gives the very photogenic Griffith an excuse to change into a variety of gorgeous costumes. The drama comes from the attempt of a gang of smugglers to obtain passports by blackmailing the consul's wife, though she manages to outwit them.[11]

Griffith enjoyed a successful career in motion pictures during the 1920s. A woman of many talents, she served as executive producer for many of her own films. Although she was seemingly capable of making the transition to talking movies, Griffith retired as an actress in 1932. She had invested wisely in real estate and eventually became a multimillionaire. She wrote a dozen books, one of which, *Papa's Delicate Condition*, became a movie starring Jackie Gleason. The most noted of her four husbands was George Preston Marshall, owner of the Washington Redskins, and Griffith wrote the (pretty awful) words to their fight song, "Hail to the Redskins."

St. Augustine boosters might have thought that the return of four movie companies in 1920 signaled a revival of motion picture making in town, but movie production in the East was in serious decline by that time. A few years later *Motion Picture Magazine* would note that at one time there had been eighty-four studios in New York City and its environs, but that number had declined to just eight by 1926—and of these only four were in use regularly. William Fox had opened a large, modern new building in

In 1919 D. W. Griffith purchased Satan's Toe, the estate of Henry M. Flagler, for use as his personal studio. Flagler's home, with the tower, stands in the center of the photo, and Griffith's studio is on the right. (From *Picture Play Magazine*)

midtown New York in 1919, but this served only to consolidate his various studios, laboratories, and offices under one roof.[12]

America's most famous director, D. W. Griffith, had built a studio in 1919 on the grounds of Henry M. Flagler's estate at Mamaroneck, New York. Since Flagler had been the major developer of St. Augustine as a winter resort, this gave the Oldest City another link to the movie industry. Griffith made his home at Mamaroneck. He was unusual as a filmmaker who moved back east from California, and perhaps it is indicative of his mindset that the films he made in the 1920s were criticized as "old-fashioned"—an interesting observation about a man who earned a reputation as a revolutionary in cinematography.

PARAMOUNT

A company of actors from Paramount arrived in St. Augustine in 1921, just as in the days of old, but it was a sign of the times that most of the actors in the group were based in California and had come east just for this production. Paramount was making the allegorical morality play *Experience* at its recently opened New York City studio. (This studio still stands as part of

George Fitzmaurice directs Richard Barthelmess in the "coming home" scene from *Experience*. Note the reflector screen the assistant uses to direct sunlight on the actor. (From *Picture Play Magazine*)

the Museum of the Moving Image—and as a monument to the last gasps of studio filmmaking in New York.)

Paramount's *Experience* was based on the play of the same name by George V. Hobart, who had also written the drama from which Pauline Fredericks' 1918 film *Madame Jealousy* was taken. George Fitzmaurice, a respected French-born director, supervised the filming. He had originally taken a dozen actors and crew to Savannah, Georgia, to shoot outdoor scenes, but found it far too cold for comfort. The playwright, Hobart, happened to be vacationing in St. Augustine at the time, and by telephone invited Fitzmaurice to come a little farther south. Thus, the Famous Players troupe arrived in mid-February and registered at the Hotel Alcazar.

The most popular of the actors was Richard Barthelmess, who had played opposite Florence Reed in *The Eternal Sin*, which had been filmed in St. Augustine in 1917. More recently Barthelmess had starred with

Lillian Gish in D. W. Griffith's *Way Down East*. As in that film, Barthelmess plays a handsome, good-hearted country boy. Here he is called Youth, and is taken to the Big City by Ambition, where he meets Experience. Soon he is seduced by Pleasure and several other evils that lurk in the Metropolis. When Youth has exhausted his slender funds, he is cast out and returns home where he finds Love, played by Marjorie Daw. The exterior scenes of "home" in the opening and closing scenes were taken in St. Augustine, on the St. Johns River, and at a potato farm in nearby Hastings.[13] The movie did not take advantage of the old Spanish buildings or Flagler's magnificent hotels in town, and thus most people in town completely missed the bustle of scene shooting.

Five years later Fitzmaurice would direct Valentino in *The Son of the Sheik*, which is widely regarded as Valentino's best performance. Fitzmaurice would continue making films on through the 1930s. Barthelmess achieved his greatest fame in the 1920s, but his career waned when talking pictures arrived, although he would fill small roles in films until 1942. Another actor in *Experience*, Reginald Denny, enjoyed the longest film career, although when talking movies came along, his stereotypical British accent confined him to supporting roles. His list of credits includes *The Lost Patrol* (1934), *Of Human Bondage* (1934), and the *Batman* television series, playing Commodore Schmidlapp (1966), his final role.

PATHÉ

In 1922 when a Pathé crew arrived to take some pictures, the *St. Augustine Record* would note, "It has been some time since St. Augustine people and visitors have seen motion pictures in the making, and the stay of these players in the city promises to be very interesting."[14] The movie was called *Speed* and used the serial format that had remained popular with Pathé since its success with *Perils of Pauline*. Charles Hutchison, an actor noted for his daring stunts, and Lucy Fox, the female lead, were at Silver Springs, Florida, taking water scenes when the rest of the company arrived in St. Augustine. The premise of *Speed* involved good guys and bad guys engaging in a running adventure from Florida through the South to the cliffs of the Hudson River, which required rapid changes in scenery. More than one hundred local folk appeared as supers when the action arrived at Fort Marion. Then, as quickly as they had arrived, the theater people departed.[15]

Advertisements for *Speed* highlighted "alligator infested swamps, historic points at St. Augustine, Fla." The fifteen-episode series evidently met expectations. A movie theater trade publication said: "As in most serials, there is much that baffles credulity, but those who follow them do not pay much attention to that part of it. The press agents promise a thrill a minute. There may not be as many as that, but there certainly are a great number of them. If your crowd wants action, this is their meat."[16]

ALL STAR COMEDIES

A year would go by before another film crew passed through town. The All Star Comedies troupe visited from its studio on Long Island to take some scenes "among the 'old Spanish ruins' for which this city is famous." Only seven people made up the party, and they checked in to the Hotel Alcazar on January 19, 1923. Their play, *So This Is Hamlet?*, is the story of two businessmen who decide to make a modern-day movie version of *Hamlet*. Some of the scenes were taken at Fort Marion. Charles Murray, a veteran slapstick comedian, headed the All Star cast. This company made a specialty of releasing a new two-reel comedy every two weeks. Murray would continue grinding out such short material through the 1920s and would still be playing small parts in feature movies during the 1930s.[17]

FAMOUS PLAYERS/PARAMOUNT

In 1924 the people of St. Augustine caught movie mania once again when word arrived that Thomas Meighan would be coming to town to film a major motion picture for Famous Players. At the time, handsome, wavy-haired Meighan was one of the most famous box office attractions in the country. He was no stranger to St. Augustine, having starred with Pauline Frederick in *Madame Jealousy* back in 1917. When he and a party of thirty-two Famous Players arrived at the Hotel Alcazar about midnight on January 10, the *St. Augustine Record* gave the news a banner headline. Another veteran of acting in St. Augustine was eight-year-old Jimmie Lapsley, who had played Pauline Frederick's baby daughter in the 1916 film *The Spider*.[18]

A few days later Meighan made personal appearances before each of the three showings of his film *Woman Proof* at the Jefferson Theatre. He told the audience about some details of how the film was made. The crowd for the final show was given as the largest attendance ever at the Jefferson. One-fourth of the receipts for the showings were donated to the St. Johns County Welfare Federation.[19]

When some of the crew returned to New York after just a few days of shooting, one of the film company managers explained that it was easier to bring in professional actors, even for just a few scenes, than to hire local people for the work. "Inexperienced people will always look into the camera and that scene is spoiled. Then after a tedious day of training they are told to appear the next day in the same clothes, but they invariably decide that they have other dresses in which they would rather appear. And since two days' work is often the same scene, this causes no end of trouble."[20]

The one and only scene planned for a St. Augustine location was a rainstorm that drowns out a bazaar but, ironically, filming was impossible because it rained almost every day the Famous Players were in town. Although the Alcazar served as home base for the theater people, most shooting took place in nearby communities within a thirty-mile radius. Their movie, *The Confidence Man* (1924), concerns a deceptive con artist, Meighan, who comes to a small town to sell worthless oil stocks to the town's rich old miser. The orange-grove town of San Mateo, located on the railroad southwest of St. Augustine, served as the small town. The village declared a holiday for the moviemakers and decked the main street with flags and bunting for the cameramen. Orange Park's railroad station received some attention. The small Episcopal church in Green Cove Springs served as another location, and a more upscale home in the Riverside neighborhood of Jacksonville also provided a setting.[21]

In the story Meighan shows some kindness to people in the small southern town in order to win their confidence, but slowly the warmth of the local folk begins to touch Meighan's deceitful heart. Then he falls in love with a local girl, played by Virginia Valli. The one scene shot in St. Augustine was made at the west end of Cincinnati Avenue in the northern part of town. A "poorhouse" had been constructed by the moviemakers' crew as the setting for a fund-raising party put on by the inmates of the poorhouse. In the story, just as all has been prepared, a downpour of rain spoils the poor people's efforts. On this occasion, the fire hoses of the St. Augustine Fire Department supplied the rain. Spectators crowded so close to the set that they ended up getting drenched along with the actors, but everyone seemed to enjoy the action. By the end of the film Meighan has given up his evil scheme, won the affection of the girl, and proven to himself that he is not the cad he thought himself to be.[22]

Paramount selected St. Augustine as one of the places for the premiere showing of *The Confidence Man* on April 20, 1924, which was considered quite an honor for a small town. People came from all the nearby towns where scenes had been filmed to see themselves on the silver screen. Unfortunately for St. Augustine, the nasty weather that had prevailed during the moviemakers' visit did nothing to enhance Florida's reputation as an alternative to California for shooting motion pictures.[23]

Toward the end of the year it seemed another film production company would come to town. Clayton D. Davis, Sterling W. Wilson, and Edward H. Griffith, principals of Pinellas Films, visited St. Augustine to scout locations for shooting *White Mice*, a movie based on Richard Harding Davis' tale of revolution in a small Caribbean island nation.[24] Established star Jacqueline Logan and up-and-comer William Powell (later of *The Thin Man* series) would be the leads. However, just as St. Augustine had stolen *Heart and Soul* from Cuba in 1917, so Cuba robbed St. Augustine of *White Mice*. Havana's El Morro castle, not Fort Marion, would serve as the fortress in the film.

In late April 1925 Jack MacCullough showed up in town with a proposition to make a "standard multiple-reel program release" that would employ local people in small parts and feature a young woman selected by vote of patrons of the Jefferson Theatre. Each ticket purchased came with a vote for a local girl of the ticket holder's choice. The Jefferson would keep a running tabulation of the leading ladies in the weeklong contest. The film *The Trickster's Fate* would be partly a travelogue highlighting St. Augustine's attractions, released as part of the "Know America" series by the Gromac Company of New York.[25] Jack MacCullough had been active on the margins of the moviemaking business in Chicago, producing a handful of films based on children's fairy tales, but his company, Gromac, was unknown to the film industry.

The Jefferson Theatre gave the contest a lot of publicity, and Agnes

Carrera emerged as the town's favorite. The theater invited everyone to come to the movies and watch Miss Carrera in the filming of an indoor scene onstage during the interval between the shows. In the next couple of days the company shot scenes at a residence on North San Marco Avenue and on the Plaza, as well as at several of the historic sites in town.[26]

On May 13 a big crowd jammed the Jefferson to see the end result of the project. The *St. Augustine Record* gave Miss Carrera high marks for her appearance and acting, but noted that the scenes of St. Augustine's attractions were "not particularly clear." The reporter excused this by saying that the film was a "pre-release print" that would be refined in the New York studio, but nothing was ever heard thereafter of the film, Gromac Company, or MacCullough.[27]

TEC ART PATHÉ

Silent filmmaking in St. Augustine did not end on that low note, however. In March 1926 James A. Fitzpatrick arrived with a small company from New York to make *Songs of Spain*, a one-reel short in the "Famous Melody" series produced by Fitzpatrick's independent company, Tec Art. These films were built around famous songs from various locales, such as Ireland and Scotland. Pathé distributed the productions and sent a musical score along with each reel of film so that musicians in the theater could synchronize their music to the pictures on the screen.[28]

St. Augustine's scenic venues stood in for Spain in the picture. Peggy Shaw, an experienced actress, played the lead role, as she had in earlier episodes in which she appeared in different costumes to fit each country. She wore a "fascinating Spanish costume" on the west lawn of the Hotel Ponce de Leon during one of the hotel's afternoon tea dances. In another scene Fitzpatrick himself acted as a Spanish lover serenading his lady seated on the balcony of the Oldest House. Fitzpatrick took shots of other "atmospheric" sites, including Fort Marion. A few local residents acted in bit parts in the play. The completed film reached theaters in June. It featured the songs *In Old Madrid, Juanita, Spanish Cavalier*, and *La Paloma*.[29]

The Famous Melody series would become a jumping-off point for James A. Fitzpatrick. He soon dropped the musical aspect of his films and began doing straight travel documentaries. His "Voice of the Globe"

Theda Bara emotes for the camera in the front garden of the Hotel Alcazar. The Hotel Casa Monica can be seen in the background. (Courtesy of St. Augustine Historical Society)

travelogues from far-flung reaches of the world became staples for MGM through the 1950s.

By the mid-1920s St. Augustine had long abandoned its aspirations to become a movie center. Instead, it was enjoying a boom based on land development and population growth. This all came crashing down with the onset of the Great Depression, and St. Augustine returned to its traditional role as a quaint old town where vacationers—now driving automobiles—stopped over for a one-day visit on their way to Miami. Today, swamped with ever-increasing waves of tourists, St. Augustine is striving valiantly to maintain its historic atmosphere.

After the passage of a century, few people are even aware that once upon a time local residents and tourists could watch giants of the silent screen fret and strut upon the stage of St. Augustine's gardens and narrow streets. The memory of visits by Tom Mix, Theda Bara, Rudolph Valentino, Oliver Hardy, Ethel Barrymore, and a host of once-famous movie stars and directors has simply evaporated like a reel of nitrate cellulose. Even the palm tree Theda Bara planted in the plaza is gone, probably killed in a hard freeze decades ago.

That's All There Is
There Isn't Any More

ETHEL BARRYMORE

ACKNOWLEDGMENTS

Lisa Bradberry, Florida film historian

James Cusick, librarian, P. K. Yonge Library, University of Florida

Leonard DeGraaf, archivist, Thomas Edison National Historical Park

Ben DiBiase, director of educational resources, Florida Historical Society

Susan Doll, professor, Ringling College of Art

Greta de Groat, professor, Stanford University

Donna L. Hill, Rudolph Valentino biographer

Nancy Kauffman, archivist, George Eastman House

Christina Lane, professor, University of Miami

Janet Lorenz, NFIS researcher, Margaret Herrick Library, Academy of Motion Picture Arts and Sciences

Robert Nawrocki, chief librarian, St. Augustine Historical Society

Thomas Rahner, actor, director, playwright of St. Augustine

Natalka Sawchuk, archivist, Thanhouser Archive, Iona College

Randy Sketvedt, Laurel and Hardy expert

Edwin Thanhouser, Thanhouser Company Film Preservation, Inc.

Charles Tingley, archivist, St. Augustine Historical Society

Debra Willis, Photo Enhancement, St. Augustine Historical Society

Joseph Yranski, film expert

APPENDIX A

MOVIES MADE IN ST. AUGUSTINE

All Love Excelling	Pathé	1914
Always in the Way	Dyreda Art Film/Metro	1915
The Arab's Bride	Thanhouser	1912
Barbary Sheep	Famous Players	1917
Bedelia and the Suffragette	Reliance	1912
Bella Donna	Famous Players	1915
Bungling Bunk's Bunco	Pathé	1914
The Butterfly	Peerless/World	1915
The Call of Her People	Metro/Columbia	1917
A Celebrated Case	Kalem	1914
The Cipher Key	Lubin	1915
The Confidence Man	Famous Players	1924
A Corner in Cotton	Metro	1916
Coughing Higgins	Johnny Ray	1917
Daughter of Destiny	Petrova	1917
The Dead Alive	Gaumont/Mutual	1916
The Debt	Lubin	1914
Destiny's Skein	Lubin	1915
The Devil's Daughter	Fox	1915
Dimples	Metro	1916
Don Caesar de Bazan	Kalem	1915
Duchess of Doubt	Metro	1917
The Education of Mr. Pipp	All Star Feature Films	1914

The Eternal Sin	Herbert Brenon Films	1917
Exile	Lasky/Paramount	1917
Experience	Paramount	1921
The First Prize	Lubin	1913
The Flight of the Duchess	Thanhouser	1916
A Florida Enchantment	Vitagraph	1914
Florida to Louisiana	Educational Film	1917
Flying to Fortune	Thanhouser	1912
A Fool There Was	Fox	1915
For Sale—A Life	Thanhouser	1912
Forgiven, or the Jack O'Diamonds	Stellar Feature Photoplay	1914
Four Feathers	Dyreda Art Film/Metro	1915
The Garden of Lies	All Star Feature Films/Alco	1914
The Girl of the Grove	Thanhouser	1912
The Golf Caddie's Dog	Thanhouser	1912
Good Pals	Pathé	1914
The Haunted Manor	Gaumont	1916
Heart and Soul	Fox	1917
Heart's Desire	Famous Players	1917
Her American Prince	Popular Film/Mutual	1916
Her Great Hour	Equitable	1916
Her Greatest Love	Fox	1917
The Hermit of Bird Island	Lubin	1915
Hidden Valley	Thanhouser	1916
Historic St. Augustine, Florida	Gaumont/Mutual	1916
Honeymoon Through Snow to Sunshine	Lubin	1910
Idols	Equitable	1916
The Image Maker of Thebes	Thanhouser	1916
In Old Florida	Kalem	1911
In the Hands of the Law	B. S. Moss	1917
The Insurrection	Lubin	1915
Into the Desert	Thanhouser	1912
The Invisible Ray	Frohman	1920
Jess: A Sister's Sacrifice	Thanhouser	1912
Jilted	Thanhouser	1912
Lady Barnacle	Metro	1917

La Tosca	Famous Players	1918
The Last Rebel	Lubin	1915
The Law of Compensation	Norma Talmadge	1917
The Law of the Land	Lasky/Paramount	1917
Let's Get a Divorce	Famous Players/Paramount	1918
Life Without Soul	Ocean Film	1915
The Lotus Woman	Kalem	1916
A Love Long Ago	Thanhouser	1912
Love's Miracle	Thanhouser	1912
The Lovely Señorita	Edison	1914
Madame Jealousy	Famous Players	1918
The Man from the Sea	Lubin	1914
The Man of God	Lubin	1915
Maternity	Brady/World	1917
The Message in the Rose	Edison	1914
The Message of the Sun Dial	Edison	1914
Miss Arabella Snaith	Thanhouser	1912
M'liss	Peerless/World	1915
The Moth and the Flame	Famous Players	1915
My Lady Incog.	Famous Players	1916
Never Again	Vim	1916
A Night at the Inn	Edison	1914
One Law for Both	Ivan Films	1917
The Oval Diamond	Thanhouser	1916
Pa's Medicine/Hazers Hazed	Thanhouser	1912
Pearl of the Punjab	Pathé	1914
Perils of Pauline (serial)	Pathé	1914
Ponce de Leon Celebration	Universal	1913
Ponce de Leon Fete	Kalem	1909
Redemption	Triumph	1917
Rejuvenation	Thanhouser	1912
The Revelation	Metro	1918
The Ring of a Spanish Grandee	Thanhouser	1912
A Romance of the Everglades	Edison	1914
Rorke's Drift	Edison	1914
The Rose of Old St. Augustine	Selig Polyscope	1911

St. Augustine	Pathé	1916
St. Augustine, Florida	Reliance	1912
St. Augustine in Motion	Day and Clark	1914
St. Augustine Pictures	M & C	1913
The Saleslady	Thanhouser	1912
The Seminole's Vengeance	Kalem	1909
The Silent Death	Edison	1914
So This Is Hamlet?	All Star Comedies	1923
The Social Highwayman	Peerless/World	1916
Songs of Spain	Tec Art	1926
Sons of a Soldier	Éclair	1913
Speed	Seitz/Pathé	1922
The Spider	Famous Players/Paramount	1916
Stolen Moments	American Cinema	1920
The Taming of Mary	Thanhouser	1912
The Telegrapher's Peril	Lubin	1915
Thais	Samuel Goldwyn	1917
Three Green Eyes	World	1919
Three Men and a Woman	Lubin	1914
To the Death	Metro	1917
Toys of Fate	Metro	1918
A Trip to Old St. Augustine	Ford Motor Co.	1917
The Undying Flame	Lasky	1917
Vengeance	World	1918
What Doris Did	Thanhouser	1916
What Happened to Jones	Brady/World	1915
When Rome Ruled	Pathé	1914
The Whisper Market	Vitagraph	1920
The White Goddess	Kalem	1915
Whom God Hath Joined	Thanhouser	1912
Women of the Desert	Lubin	1913
The World and His Wife	Cosmopolitan/Paramount	1920
The Yellow Menace	Serial Film	1916
The Zingara	Aetna	1914

APPENDIX B

ACTORS IN ST. AUGUSTINE MOVIES

Herbert Abbe	*The Silent Death*	Edison	1914
	The Lovely Señorita	Edison	1914
Arthur Albertson	*The White Goddess*	Kalem	1915
	The Lotus Woman	Kalem	1916
Martin Alsop	*Her Great Hour*	Equitable	1916
Edwin August	*The Social Highwayman*	Peerless/World	1916
Stewart Baird	*The Moth and the Flame*	Famous Players	1915
Sue Balfore	*Life Without Soul*	Ocean Film	1915
Theda Bara	*A Fool There Was*	Fox	1915
	The Devil's Daughter	Fox	1915
	Her Greatest Love	Fox	1917
	Heart and Soul	Fox	1917
Mathilde Baring	*The Haunted Manor*	Gaumont	1916
Bradley Barker	*The Moth and the Flame*	Famous Players	1915
	Her American Prince	Popular Film/Mutual	1916
Ethel Barrymore	*The Call of Her People*	Metro/Columbia	1917
Richard Barthelmess	*The Eternal Sin*	Herbert Brenon Films	1917
	Experience	Paramount	1921
Arthur Bauer	*The Oval Diamond*	Thanhouser	1916
Digby Bell	*The Education of Mr. Pipp*	All Star Feature Films	1914
Yale Benner	*The Silent Death*	Edison	1914
Carlyle Blackwell	*Three Green Eyes*	World	1919

Alice Brady	*Maternity*	Brady/World	1917
Clifford Bruce	*When Rome Ruled*	Pathé	1914
	The Devil's Daughter	Fox	1915
Edna Brun	*The Education of Mr. Pipp*	All Star Feature Films	1914
Charles Bryant	*Toys of Fate*	Metro	1918
	The Revelation	Metro	1918
Charles Bunnell	*Good Pals*	Pathé	1914
	When Rome Ruled	Pathé	1914
	Pearl of the Punjab	Pathé	1914
William Burt	*The Image Maker of Thebes*	Thanhouser	1916
Frederick Burton	*Forgiven, or the Jack O'Diamonds*	Stellar Feature Photoplay	1914
A. H. Busby	*When Rome Ruled*	Pathé	1914
George Busby	*Pearl of the Punjab*	Pathé	1914
W. Lawton Butt	*Don Caesar de Bazan*	Kalem	1915
Robert Cain	*My Lady Incog.*	Famous Players	1916
Edwin Carewe	*The First Prize*	Lubin	1913
	Women of the Desert	Lubin	1913
Frank Carlyle	*Perils of Pauline*	Pathé	1914
Barbara Castleton	*Vengeance*	World	1918
Mary Charleston	*What Happened to Jones*	Brady/World	1915
Ruth Clifford	*The Invisible Ray*	Frohman	1920
Robert Clugston	*The Haunted Manor*	Gaumont	1916
Franklin P. Coates	*Always in the Way*	Dyreda Art Film/Metro	1915
William A. Cohill	*Life Without Soul*	Ocean Film	1915
Guy Coombs	*A Celebrated Case*	Kalem	1914
	The White Goddess	Kalem	1915
Bigelow Cooper	*A Night at the Inn*	Edison	1914
	The Silent Death	Edison	1914
Pedro de Cordoba	*Barbary Sheep*	Famous Players	1917
	The World and His Wife	Cosmopolitan/Paramount	1920
Armand Cortes	*The Yellow Menace*	Serial Film	1916
Lucy Cotton	*Life Without Soul*	Ocean Film	1915
Marguerite Courtot	*The Dead Alive*	Gaumont/Mutual	1916
George Cowl	*The Zingara*	Aetna	1914

Jane Cowl	*The Garden of Lies*	All Star Feature Films/ Alco	1914
Nell Craig	*Pearl of the Punjab*	Pathé	1914
	When Rome Ruled	Pathé	1914
James Cruze	*The Arab's Bride*	Thanhouser	1912
	Into the Desert	Thanhouser	1912
	Jess: A Sister's Sacrifice	Thanhouser	1912
	The Ring of a Spanish Grandee	Thanhouser	1912
	For Sale—A Life	Thanhouser	1912
	Whom God Hath Joined	Thanhouser	1912
	The Golf Caddie's Dog	Thanhouser	1912
	Rejuvenation	Thanhouser	1912
Wm. Robert Daley	*Forgiven, or the Jack O'Diamonds*	Stellar Feature Photoplay	1914
Viola Dana	*Lady Barnacle*	Metro	1917
Belle Daube	*The Education of Mr. Pipp*	All Star Feature Films	1914
Dorothy Davenport	*The Butterfly*	Peerless/World	1915
Marjorie Daw	*Experience*	Paramount	1921
Hazel Dawn	*My Lady Incog.*	Famous Players	1916
Bert Delaney	*What Doris Did*	Thanhouser	1916
Reginald Denny	*Experience*	Paramount	1921
Arthur Donaldson	*Her American Prince*	Popular Film/Mutual	1916
Marie Doro	*Heart's Desire*	Famous Players	1917
Paul Doucet	*The Devil's Daughter*	Fox	1915
Sidney Drew	*A Florida Enchantment*	Vitagraph	1914
Henry Driscole	*The Education of Mr. Pipp*	All Star Feature Films	1914
Jack Drumier	*Vengeance*	World	1918
June Elvidge	*Three Green Eyes*	World	1919
Fred Esmelton	*Law of Compensation*	Norma Talmadge	1917
Howard Estabrook	*M'Liss*	Peerless/World	1915
	Four Feathers	Dyreda Art Film/Metro	1915
	The Butterfly	Peerless/World	1915
Arthur Evans	*Four Feathers*	Dyreda Art Film/Metro	1915
Madge Evans	*Vengeance*	World	1918

Elsie Ferguson	*Barbary Sheep*	Famous Players	1917
Herbert Fortier	*The Debt*	Lubin	1914
	The Telegrapher's Peril	Lubin	1915
	The Last Rebel	Lubin	1915
Lucy Fox	*Speed*	Seitz/Pathé	1922
Pauline Frederick	*Bella Donna*	Famous Players	1915
	The Spider	Famous Players/Paramount	1916
	Madame Jealousy	Famous Players	1918
	La Tosca	Famous Players	1918
Edwin Forsberg	*Forgiven, or the Jack O'Diamonds*	Stellar Feature Photoplay	1914
Caroline French	*Forgiven, or the Jack O'Diamonds*	Stellar Feature Photoplay	1914
Margaret Gale	*The Yellow Menace*	Serial Film	1916
Mary Garden	*Thais*	Samuel Goldwyn	1917
Charles K. Gerrard	*The World and His Wife*	Cosmopolitan/Paramount	1920
Barbara Gilroy	*The Oval Diamond*	Thanhouser	1916
Gaston Glass	*The World and His Wife*	Cosmopolitan/Paramount	1920
Harris Gordon	*What Doris Did*	Thanhouser	1916
	The Image Maker of Thebes	Thanhouser	1916
	The Oval Diamond	Thanhouser	1916
Robert Gray	*The Flight of the Duchess*	Thanhouser	1916
Joseph Graybill	*Girl of the Grove*	Thanhouser	1912
	For Sale—A Life	Thanhouser	1912
	The Ring of a Spanish Grandee	Thanhouser	1912
Evelyn Greeley	*Three Green Eyes*	World	1919
Mabel Green	*Always in the Way*	Dyreda Art Film/Metro	1915
Kempton Greene	*Three Men and a Woman*	Lubin	1914
	The Debt	Lubin	1914
	The Man from the Sea	Lubin	1914
	Destiny's Skein	Lubin	1915
	The Man of God	Lubin	1915

	The Telegrapher's Peril	Lubin	1915
	The Last Rebel	Lubin	1915
Doris Grey	What Doris Did	Thanhouser	1916
Corinne Griffith	The Whisper Market	Vitagraph	1920
Harry Gripp	The Silent Death	Edison	1914
	The Lovely Señorita	Edison	1914
	Rorke's Drift	Edison	1914
Philip Hahn	The Garden of Lies	All Star Feature Films/ Alco	1914
J. A. Hall	The Yellow Menace	Serial Film	1916
Mahlon Hamilton	Exile	Lasky/Paramount	1917
Oliver Hardy	Never Again	Vim	1916
Lumsden Hare	Barbary Sheep	Famous Players	1917
Riley Hatch	When Rome Ruled	Pathé	1914
Arthur Hauer	The Image Maker of Thebes	Thanhouser	1916
Ormi Hawley	The First Prize	Lubin	1913
	Women of the Desert	Lubin	1913
	Destiny's Skein	Lubin	1915
	The Man of God	Lubin	1915
	The Telegrapher's Peril	Lubin	1915
	The Last Rebel	Lubin	1915
	The Insurrection	Lubin	1915
	Her American Prince	Popular Film/Mutual	1916
	The Social Highwayman	Peerless/World	1916
Lillian Herbert	The Silent Death	Edison	1914
Doris Heywood	The Devil's Daughter	Fox	1915
Ruby Hoffman	Her American Prince	Popular Film/Mutual	1916
Thomas Holding	Bella Donna	Famous Players	1915
Alice Hollister	A Celebrated Case	Kalem	1914
	Don Caesar de Bazan	Kalem	1915
	The Lotus Woman	Kalem	1916
Gerda Holmes	Her Great Hour	Equitable	1916
Jack Hopkins	Life Without Soul	Ocean Film	1915
George Howard	The Whisper Market	Vitagraph	1920

Hazel Hubbard	*Destiny's Skein*	Lubin	1915
Gladys Hulette	*What Doris Did*	Thanhouser	1916
	The Flight of the Duchess	Thanhouser	1916
Charles Hutchison	*Speed*	Seitz/Pathé	1922
Kate Jepson	*The Education of Mr. Pipp*	All Star Feature Films	1914
Marcus Jones	*The Image Maker of Thebes*	Thanhouser	1916
Morgan Jones	*What Doris Did*	Thanhouser	1916
Edward José	*A Fool There Was*	Fox	1915
	Perils of Pauline	Pathé	1914
Alice Joyce	*A Celebrated Case*	Kalem	1914
	The White Goddess	Kalem	1915
Mary Keane	*The Debt*	Lubin	1914
Charles Kent	*A Florida Enchantment*	Vitagraph	1914
Carlton King	*The Lovely Señorita*	Edison	1914
	Rorke's Drift	Edison	1914
Florence La Badie	*The Arab's Bride*	Thanhouser	1912
	The Girl of the Grove	Thanhouser	1912
	Jess: A Sister's Sacrifice	Thanhouser	1912
	Whom God Hath Joined	Thanhouser	1912
	Jilted	Thanhouser	1912
	The Ring of a Spanish Grandee	Thanhouser	1912
	A Love Long Ago	Thanhouser	1912
	Rejuvenation	Thanhouser	1912
	What Doris Did	Thanhouser	1916
Walter Law	*Heart and Soul*	Fox	1917
Pierre LeMay	*Her Great Hour*	Equitable	1916
Anne Leonard	*The Lovely Señorita*	Edison	1914
Julian L'Estrange	*Bella Donna*	Famous Players	1915
James Levering	*The Dead Alive*	Gaumont/Mutual	1916
Jessie Lewis	*The Butterfly*	Peerless/World	1915
Ethel Lloyd	*A Florida Enchantment*	Vitagraph	1914
Frank Losee	*La Tosca*	Famous Players	1918
	Madame Jealousy	Famous Players	1918

Montagu Love	Vengeance	World	1918
	Three Green Eyes	World	1919
	The World and His Wife	Cosmopolitan/Paramount	1920
Oscar A. C. Lund	M'Liss	Peerless/World	1915
Anna Luther	Three Men and a Woman	Lubin	1914
	The Man from the Sea	Lubin	1914
	The Debt	Lubin	1914
Richard Lynn	Her Great Hour	Equitable	1916
Fred Mace	What Happened to Jones	Brady/World	1915
J. E. Mackin	Don Caesar de Bazan	Kalem	1915
Elsie MacLeod	A Romance of the Everglades	Edison	1914
	The Silent Death	Edison	1914
	The Message of the Sun Dial	Edison	1914
	The Lovely Señorita	Edison	1914
	Madame Jealousy	Famous Players	1918
George MacQuarre	Vengeance	World	1918
	The Whisper Market	Vitagraph	1920
Tom Mahoney	Coughing Higgins	Johnny Ray	1917
George Majeroni	My Lady Incog.	Famous Players	1916
Florence Malone	The Yellow Menace	Serial Film	1916
Josephine Marshall	Life Without Soul	Ocean Film	1915
Rosita Marstini	When Rome Ruled	Pathé	1914
Sydney Mason	The Dead Alive	Gaumont/Mutual	1916
Christine Mayo	The Zingara	Aetna	1914
Molly McIntyre	Her Great Hour	Equitable	1916
Thomas Meighan	Madame Jealousy	Famous Players	1918
	The Confidence Man	Famous Players	1924
Lois Meredith	In the Hands of the Law	B. S. Moss	1917
Earl Metcalfe	Women of the Desert	Lubin	1913
	Three Men and a Woman	Lubin	1914
	The Debt	Lubin	1914
	The Man from the Sea	Lubin	1914
	Destiny's Skein	Lubin	1915
	The Man of God	Lubin	1915
	The Telegrapher's Peril	Lubin	1915

	The Last Rebel	Lubin	1915
	The Insurrection	Lubin	1915
Harry Millard	*Don Caesar de Bazan*	Kalem	1915
	The Lotus Woman	Kalem	1916
John Miltern	*Experience*	Paramount	1921
Mary Miles Minter	*Always in the Way*	Dyreda Art Film/Metro	1915
Beatrice Moreland	*Good Pals*	Pathé	1914
Jane Morrow	*A Florida Enchantment*	Vitagraph	1914
Charles Murray	*So This Is Hamlet?*	All Star Comedies	1923
Alla Nazimova	*Toys of Fate*	Metro	1918
Evelyn Nesbit	*Redemption*	Triumph	1917
Eugene Ormond	*Bella Donna*	Famous Players	1915
Paul Panzer	*Perils of Pauline*	Pathé	1914
	When Rome Ruled	Pathé	1914
Madelene Pardee	*The Butterfly*	Peerless/World	1915
Barnett Parker	*The Flight of the Duchess*	Thanhouser	1916
Henry Pemberton	*The Haunted Manor*	Gaumont	1916
	The Dead Alive	Gaumont/Mutual	1916
Walter Percival	*Coughing Higgins*	Johnny Ray	1917
Olga Petrova	*The Undying Flame*	Lasky	1917
	Exile	Lasky/Paramount	1917
	To the Death	Metro	1917
	Daughter of Destiny	Petrova	1917
Herbert Prior	*The Message in the Rose*	Edison	1914
	The Message of the Sun Dial	Edison	1914
	The Silent Death	Edison	1914
	A Night at the Inn	Edison	1914
Fred Radcliffe	*The Butterfly*	Peerless/World	1915
Adele Ray	*The Moth and the Flame*	Famous Players	1915
Emma Ray	*Coughing Higgins*	Johnny Ray	1917
Johnny Ray	*Coughing Higgins*	Johnny Ray	1917
Florence Reed	*The Eternal Sin*	Herbert Brenon Films	1917
Hamilton Revelle	*Thais*	Samuel Goldwyn	1917
Marguerite Risser	*Good Pals*	Pathé	1914
Gertrude Robinson	*The Haunted Manor*	Gaumont	1916

Alma Rubens	*The World and His Wife*	Cosmopolitan/Paramount	1920
William Russell	*The Arab's Bride*	Thanhouser	1912
	Girl of the Grove	Thanhouser	1912
	Into the Desert	Thanhouser	1912
	Jess: A Sister's Sacrifice	Thanhouser	1912
	For Sale—A Life	Thanhouser	1912
	Jilted	Thanhouser	1912
	The Ring of a Spanish Grandee	Thanhouser	1912
	A Love Long Ago	Thanhouser	1912
	Rejuvenation	Thanhouser	1912
	The Garden of Lies	All Star Feature Films/ Alco	1914
Jose Sadler	*What Happened to Jones*	Brady/World	1915
Laura Sawyer	*Four Feathers*	Dyreda Art Film/Metro	1915
Earl Schenck	*The Haunted Manor*	Gaumont	1916
Walter Seymour	*Pearl of the Punjab*	Pathé	1914
	When Rome Ruled	Pathé	1914
	Bungling Bink's Bunco	Pathé	1914
Alex Shannon	*Barbary Sheep*	Famous Players	1917
	Stolen Moments	American Cinema	1920
William Shay	*The Eternal Sin*	Herbert Brenon Films	1917
Iva Shepard	*The Haunted Manor*	Gaumont	1916
Jack Sherrill	*The Invisible Ray*	Frohman	1920
Marguerite Snow	*The Girl of the Grove*	Thanhouser	1912
	Into the Desert	Thanhouser	1912
	Jess: A Sister's Sacrifice	Thanhouser	1912
	For Sale—A Life	Thanhouser	1912
	Whom God Hath Joined	Thanhouser	1912
	Jilted	Thanhouser	1912
	The Ring of a Spanish Grandee	Thanhouser	1912
Percy D. Standing	*Life Without Soul*	Ocean Film	1915
Wyndham Standing	*Exile*	Lasky/Paramount	1917
Edwin Stevens	*The Yellow Menace*	Serial Film	1916

Grace Stevens	*A Florida Enchantment*	Vitagraph	1914
Edith Storey	*A Florida Enchantment*	Vitagraph	1914
Julia Stuart	*The Butterfly*	Peerless/World	1915
Mabel Taliaferro	*When Rome Ruled*	Pathé	1914
Norma Talmadge	*Law of Compensation*	Norma Talmadge	1917
Lilyan Tashman	*Experience*	Paramount	1921
Barbara Tennant	*M'Liss*	Peerless/World	1915
	The Butterfly	Peerless/World	1915
Olive Trevor	*The Haunted Manor*	Mutual	1916
Ernest Truex	*When Rome Ruled*	Pathé	1914
Mabel Trunnelle	*The Message of the Sun Dial*	Edison	1914
	The Message in the Rose	Edison	1914
	A Night at the Inn	Edison	1914
	The Lovely Señorita	Edison	1914
	Rorke's Drift	Edison	1914
Richard Tucker	*The Message in the Rose*	Edison	1914
	Rorke's Drift	Edison	1914
Madame Valkyrien	*The Image Maker of Thebes*	Thanhouser	1916
(Adele Freed/	*Hidden Valley*	Thanhouser	1916
Baroness Dewitz)			
Virginia Valli	*The Confidence Man*	Famous Players	1924
William Wadsworth	*The Lovely Señorita*	Edison	1914
Irene Warfield	*Four Feathers*	Dyreda Art Film/Metro	1915
Emmy Wehlen	*Duchess of Doubt*	Metro 1917	
Pearl White	*Perils of Pauline*	Pathé	1914
Claire Whitney	*Heart and Soul*	Fox	1917
Lillian Wiggins	*Pearl of the Punjab*	Pathé	1914
	Bungling Bink's Bunco	Pathé	1914
Crane Wilbur	*Perils of Pauline*	Pathé	1914
Edna Mae Wilson	*The Education of Mr. Pipp*	All Star Feature Films	1914

NOTES

CHAPTER 1. FIRST EXPOSURES, 1906–1911

1. Smith, *Two Reels*, 32.

2. "News Notes," *(Jacksonville) Florida Times-Union*, January 5, 1898, 2.

3. "Casino Opening," *The Tatler* 7, no. 2 (January 22, 1898): 15.

4. "The Casino," *The Tatler* 15, no. 11 (March 17, 1906): 20.

5. "At the Theater," *St. Augustine Evening Record*, April 3, 1907, 4.

6. "Local Notes," *St. Augustine Evening Record*, August 25, 1908, 4; and September 1, 1908, 4.

7. "Local Notes," *St. Augustine Evening Record*, September 11, 1908, 4.

8. "Local Notes," *St. Augustine Evening Record*, August 8, 1908, 5; September 4, 1908, 4; and September 5, 1908, 4.

9. "Opening of the New Plaza Theater," *St. Augustine Evening Record*, November 24, 1908, 5.

10. "New Orpheum Theatre," *St. Augustine Evening Record*, June 8, 1909, 4; "Opening of New Orpheum Theatre," *St. Augustine Evening Record*, June 9, 1909, 5.

11. "Progress of the Theater Project," *St. Augustine Evening Record*, June 12, 1907, 1; "Jefferson, Name of New Theater," *St. Augustine Evening Record*, October 21, 1907, 1.

12. "Jefferson Theatre Opens," *St. Augustine Evening Record*, February 23, 1909, 1; "Jeffersons Formally Open Jefferson Theatre," *St. Augustine Evening Record*, September 24, 1909, 1.

13. Bean, *First Hollywood*, 44–48.

14. "The Seminole's Vengeance," *Moving Picture World* 4, no. 9 (February 27, 1909): 279.

15. "Ponce de Leon Moving Pictures," *St. Augustine Evening Record*, May 13, 1909, 5; "Ponce de Leon Celebration Moving Pictures," *St. Augustine Evening Record*, May 14, 1909, 4; "The Ponce de Leon Fete," *Moving Picture World* 4, no. 20 (May 15, 1909): 623.

16. "Taking Moving Pictures," *St. Augustine Evening Record*, January 12, 1910, 4; "Interesting Pictures," *St. Augustine Evening Record*, January 13, 1910, 1; "Honeymoon Through Snow to Sunshine," *Moving Picture World* 6, no. 7 (February 19, 1910): 269.

17. "Through Snow to Sunshine," *Variety* 17, no. 12 (February 26, 1910): 15.

18. Bean, *First Hollywood*, 70.

19. "Plaza Theater," *St. Augustine Evening Record*, March 22, 1910, 8.

20. "In Old Florida," *St. Augustine Evening Record*, May 12, 1911, 4; "In Old Florida," *Motography* 5, no. 5 (May 1911): 97.

21. "The Rose of Old St. Augustine," *St. Augustine Evening Record*, June 23, 1911, 5; Mix, *Tom Mix*; "Louella Maxam," *Motion Picture News Studio Directory* 2, no. 1 (April 12, 1917): 103.

22. "The Rose of Old St. Augustine," *Moving Picture World* 8, no. 11 (June 17, 1911): 1386.

23. "The Rose of Old St. Augustine," *Motography* 5, no. 6 (June 1911): 148. This film survives in the EYE Museum in Amsterdam and can be viewed on YouTube.

CHAPTER 2. THE THANHOUSER SEASON, 1912

1. Sargent, *Techniques*, 260.

2. "Moving Picture Company Is Here," *St. Augustine Evening Record*, January 15, 1912, 1; "Thanhouser Two a Week," *Moving Picture World* 11, no. 7 (February 17, 1912): 532.

3. "Thanhouser Two a Week," *Moving Picture World* 11, no. 8 (February 24, 1912): 638.

4. "Thanhouser Two a Week," *Moving Picture World* 11, no. 12 (March 23, 1912): 1022, 1102.

5. "Thanhouser Two a Week," *Moving Picture World* 11, no. 13 (March 30, 1912): 1122; Bowers, *Thanhouser Films*.

6. "Local Happenings," *St. Augustine Evening Record*, February 16, 1912, 4, 5.

7. "The Saleslady," *Moving Picture News* 5, no. 17 (April 27, 1912): 21.

8. "The Golf Caddie's Dog," *Moving Picture News* 5, no. 10 (March 9, 1912): 40.

9. "Thanhouser Two a Week," *Moving Picture World* 12, no. 3 (April 20, 1912): 186.

10. "Thanhouser Two a Week," *Moving Picture World* 12, no. 7 (May 18, 1912): 586, 636.

11. "Moving Picture Troupe Leaves," *St. Augustine Evening Record*, February 29, 1912, 1.

CHAPTER 3. MOVIES DISCOVER ST. AUGUSTINE, 1913–1914

1. "The First Prize," *Moving Picture World* 15, no. 11 (March 15, 1913): 1042.

2. "Women of the Desert," *Moving Picture World* 16, no. 2 (April 12, 1913): 164.

3. "At the Orpheum," *St. Augustine Record*, May 26, 1913, 5.

4. "Éclair Company Here," *St. Augustine Record*, March 17, 1913, 1.

5. "Sons of a Soldier," *Moving Picture News* 7, no. 17 (April 26, 1913): 23–24.

6. "Silent Movies in St. Augustine," *St. Augustine Record*, March 27, 1951, 8.

7. "Scenes of the Celebration," *St. Augustine Record*, April 15, 1913, 5.

8. "Pathe Freres Co." *St. Augustine Record*, October 16, 1913, 5.

9. "New Pathe Studio," *Motion Picture News* 8, no. 18 (November 8, 1913): 35.

10. "Pathe Animal Pictures," *Motion Picture News* 8, no. 16 (October 25, 1913): 39; "Training Lions and Tigers," *Reel Life*, November 29, 1913, 8–9.

11. "Fierce Beasts on Exhibition," *St. Augustine Record*, October 18, 1913, 5; "Paul Bourgeois Wild Animal Show," *St. Augustine Record*, October 22, 1913, 5; "Hundreds Go to Neptune Park," *St. Augustine Record*, November 7, 1913, 1.

12. "Pathe Company," *St. Augustine Record*, November 21, 1913, 1; "Wild Animals," *St. Augustine Record*, December 12, 1913, 1; "Walter Seymour Injured," *St. Augustine Record*, January 9, 1914, 1.

13. "Motion Pictures in the Southland," *Florida Times-Union*, March 1, 1914, Sunday supplement, n.p.

14. "Local News," *St. Augustine Record*, November 25, 1913; "Taking Hindu Picture," *St. Augustine Record*, December 19, 1913, 1.

15. "Is the Short Length Film Doomed?" *Motion Picture News* 8, no. 16 (October 25, 1913): 14.

16. "Motion Pictures in the Southland," *Florida Times-Union*, March 1, 1914, Sunday supplement, n.p.

17. "When Rome Ruled," *Motion Picture News* 10, no. 4 (August 1, 1914): 50.

18. "Lions and Rams," *Movie Pictorial* 1, no. 9 (July 4, 1914): 29.

19. "Local News," *St. Augustine Record*, July 30, 1914, 4; "At the Orpheum," *St. Augustine Record*, September 22, 1915, 4.

20. "Brevities of the Business," *Motography* 11, no. 3 (February 7, 1914): 108.

21. "World Famous Pathe Stars Arrive," *St. Augustine Record*, February 25, 1914, 1.

22. "Pauline Makes Bow," *Motography* 11, no. 7 (April 4, 1914): 217.

23. "Pathe to Take Air Movie Here," *St. Augustine Record*, February 23, 1914, 8; "Aviator Gray Here," *St. Augustine Record*, February 28, 1914, 1; "Movie at Baseball Field," *St. Augustine Record*, March 7, 1914, 4.

24. "Local News," *St. Augustine Record*, April 24, 1914, 4; "Perils of Pauline," *Motion Picture News* 9, no. 15 (April 18, 1914): 41.

25. "Takes Remarkable Picture," *Motography* 11, no. 9 (May 2, 1914): 292.

26. "Pathe Company Here to Stay," *St. Augustine Record*, March 13, 1914, 1; "Pathe Company Leases Site," *St. Augustine Record*, April 3, 1914, 1; "Pathe Company Off for North," *St. Augustine Record*, May 1, 1914, 1.

27. "Taking Hindu Picture," *St. Augustine Record*, December 19, 1913, 1; "In the Movie World," *St. Augustine Record*, November 4, 1916, 4; "Local Movie Star Enters the Army," *St. Augustine Record*, July 10, 1918, 4; "At the Jefferson," *St. Augustine Record*, January 16, 1919, 5; "Local Man in Today's Picture," *St. Augustine Record*, June 21, 1923, 4; "St. Augustine Boy," *St. Augustine Record*, October 11, 1924, 4; "Silent Movies in St. Augustine," *St. Augustine Record*, March 27, 1951, 8.

28. "Edison Company Taking Pictures," *St. Augustine Record*, November 21, 1913, 1; "Edison Movie Players in City," *St. Augustine Record*, December 9, 1913, 1.

29. "At the Orpheum," *St. Augustine Record*, August 29, 1914, 5.

30. "The Message of the Sun Dial," *Kinetogram* 9, no. 12 (January 15, 1914): 7.

31. "Silent Movies in St. Augustine," *St. Augustine Record*, March 27, 1951, 8.

32. "Staging African Picture at Beach," *St. Augustine Record*, December 19, 1913, 1, 4, 7; "Local News," *St. Augustine Record*, January 19, 1914, 4; "Local News," *St. Augustine Record*, April 20, 1914, 4.

33. "Local News," *St. Augustine Record*, April 24, 1914, 4; "Perils of Pauline," *Motion Picture News* 9, no. 15 (April 18, 1914): 41.

34. "All Stars at Work," *St. Augustine Record*, January 8, 1914, 1; "Digby Bell in 'Mr. Pipp' Coming Soon," *Motion Picture News* 10, no. 20 (November 21, 1914): 28.

35. "All Star Players Coming," *St. Augustine Record*, November 20, 1914, 4.

36. "Forgiven, or the Jack O'Diamonds," *Moving Picture World* 20, no. 4 (April 25, 1914): 501.

37. "A Celebrated Case," *Moving Picture World* 19, no. 7 (February 14, 1914): 814.

38. "St. Augustine Ideal," *St. Augustine Record*, February 28, 1914, 1.

39. "St. Augustine Popular for Film Making," *Florida Times-Union*, March 2, 1914, 11.

40. "Movie Co. at Alcazar," *St. Augustine Record*, March 3, 1914, 4.

41. "At the Orpheum," *St. Augustine Record*, August 2, 1914, 5; and August 6, 1914, 5.

42. "At the Orpheum," *St. Augustine Record*, August 26, 1914, 5.

43. "Kempton Greene, by Himself," *Moving Picture World* 25, no. 5 (July 31, 1915): 823.

44. "Will Blow Up Vessel," *St. Augustine Record*, April 10, 1914, 1; "Will Blow Up Big Yacht," *St. Augustine Record*, April 13, 1914, 1; "Proves Difficult to Burn Yacht," *St. Augustine Record*, April 16, 1914, 1; "Lubin Sinks Yacht," *Motography* 11, no. 11 (May 30, 1914): 390.

45. "Expensive Films," *Movie Pictorial* 1 (May 30, 1914): 28; "Yacht Sunk," *Motion Picture News* 10, no. 23 (December 12, 1914): 31; "The Orpheum," *St. Augustine Record*, January 26, 1915, 4.

46. "Lubin Company through Work," *St. Augustine Record*, May 9, 1914, 8.

47. "Vitagraph Players Arrive," *St. Augustine Record*, April 14, 1914, 1.

48. James McGuire to William Beardsley, May 5, 1914, McGuire Letterbook, Flagler College.

49. Brasell, "Seed for Change"; Bean and Negra, "Queer Career of Jim Crow."

50. "Vitagraph Company," *St. Augustine Record*, April 6, 1914, 1; "Hydro-Bullet Strikes Skiff," *St. Augustine Record*, April 20, 1914, 1.

51. "Silent Movies in St. Augustine," *St. Augustine Record*, March 27, 1951, 8.

52. "Vitagraph Company Leaves," *St. Augustine Record*, May 12, 1914, 1; "Vitagraph Company Off," *St. Augustine Record*, May 15, 1914, 1.

53. Hope, *Moving Picture Girls*, 65.

54. Ibid., 63, 65–68, 78.

1. "Box Office Company to Return," *St. Augustine Record*, November 30, 1914, 4.

2. "A Fool There Was," *Moving Picture World* 23, no. 5 (January 30, 1915): 677.

3. "A Fool There Was," *Motion Picture News*, January 2, 1915, 77.

4. "Famous All Star Players Here," *St. Augustine Record*, November 21, 1914, 1; "All Star People at Work," *St. Augustine Record*, November 23, 1914, 4; "All Star Company Leaves," *St. Augustine Record*, December 1, 1914, 4.

5. "The Garden of Lies," *Photoplay* 7, no. 4 (March 1915): 43–52.

6. "Timely Picture Topics," *New York Clipper* 62, no. 45 (December 19, 1914): 10.

7. "Other Jacksonville Notes," *Moving Picture World* 23, no. 4 (January 23, 1915): 541; "The Butterfly," *Moving Picture World* 24, no. 6 (May 8, 1915): 854; "Orpheum Theatre," *St. Augustine Record*, September 16, 1915, 3.

8. "M'Liss," *Moving Picture World* 23, no. 11 (March 13, 1915): 1616; "Orpheum Theatre," *St. Augustine Record*, September 9, 1915, 3.

9. "Florida for the Movies," *St. Augustine Record*, January 12, 1915, 5.

10. "In Florida Studios," *Moving Picture World* 23, no. 6 (February 6, 1915): 850; "The Orpheum," *St. Augustine Record*, April 17, 1915, 5.

11. "New York Actor Plays the Lead," *St. Augustine Record*, April 1, 1915, 5; "Four Feathers," *Moving Picture World* 24, no. 10 (June 5, 1915): 1621.

12. "Actor Poses As Oriental Merchant," *St. Augustine Record*, April 3, 1915, 4.

13. "Always in the Way," *Motion Picture News* 12, no. 1 (July 10, 1915): 75; "Animal Pictures Taken," *St. Augustine Record*, March 27, 1915, 1; "Movie Actors Do Risky Work," *St. Augustine Record*, March 29, 1915, 1.

14. "Dyreda Studio," *Variety* 38, no. 13 (May 28, 1915): 17.

15. "The Moth and the Flame," *Motion Picture News* 11, no. 19 (May 15, 1915): 3; "Jefferson Theatre," *St. Augustine Record*, June 18, 1915, 5.

16. "Lubin Company Here for Three Months' Work," *St. Augustine Record*, January 11, 1915, 1; "Lubinites Off for the South," *Motography* 8, no. 4 (January 23, 1915), 118; "St. Augustine and the Movies," *St. Augustine Record*, February 17, 1915, 2.

17. "The Hermit of Bird Island," *Moving Picture World* 23, no. 9 (February 27, 1915): 1338; "Orpheum Theatre," *St. Augustine Record*, April 19, 1915, 5.

18. "She Made Suicide Scene," *Florida Times-Union*, February 5, 1967, clipping, silent film file, St. Augustine Historical Society.

19. "Clever Screen Work," *St. Augustine Record*, March 8, 1915, 1.

20. "She Made Suicide Scene," *St. Augustine Record*, February 5, 1967, 12.

21. "Air and Sea Thrills," *Picture Play Weekly* 1, no. 2 (April 17, 1915): 24.

22. W. Livingston Larned, "Penned at Random," *St. Augustine Record*, April 19, 1915, 2.

23. W. Livingston Larned, "Penned at Random," *St. Augustine Record*, March 31, 1915, 2.

24. W. Livingston Larned, "Penned at Random," *St. Augustine Record*, April 16, 1915, 2.

25. "The Man of God," *Moving Picture World* 26, no. 3 (October 23, 1915): 664.

26. "Lubin Company Not Going to Havana," *St. Augustine Record*, February 16, 1915, 1; "Terwilliger Making 'Cave Man' Picture," *Moving Picture World* 23, no. 8 (February 20, 1915): 1148; "Reconstructing Anastasia," *Photoplay* 7, no. 6 (May 1915): 122.

27. "At the Jefferson," *St. Augustine Record*, July 19, 1915, 5; "The Insurrection," *Photoplay* 8, no. 3 (August 1915): 124–27.

28. "George Terwilliger," *Moving Picture World* 27, no. 11 (March 18, 1916): 1843.

29. Bean, *First Hollywood*, 66; "The White Goddess," *Motography* 13, no. 11 (March 13, 1915): 417; "A Romance of the Orient," *Photoplay* 7, no. 6 (May 1915): 27–29.

30. "Spanish Feature Film," *St. Augustine Record*, May 14, 1915, 1; "Don Caesar de Bazan," *Moving Picture World* 25, no. 3 (July 17, 1915): 506.

31. "Ocean Film Company Formed," *Moving Picture World* 26, no. 8 (November 13, 1915): 1316; "Ocean Company's First Film," *Motography* 14, no. 21 (November 20, 1915): 1054.

32. "Life Without Soul," *Motography* 14, no. 23 (December 4, 1915): 1194.

33. "Life Without Soul," *Moving Picture World* 26, no. 9 (December 4, 1915): 1846.

34. "Life Without Soul," *Motion Picture News* 13, no. 4 (January 29, 1916): 536; "Ocean Film Takes 'Life Without Soul' to Court," *Motion Picture News* 13, no. 6 (February 12, 1916): 840; "Life Without Soul," *Moving Picture World* 28, no. 6 (May 6, 1916): 996.

35. "The Fox Film Company," *St. Augustine Record*, May 17, 1915, 8; "Sharks and Snakes," *Motion Picture News* 11, no. 23 (June 12, 1915): 46.

36. "Fox Film Company Left," *St. Augustine Record*, May 25, 1915, 4.

37. "Theda Bara and Company Go South," *Motion Picture News* 11, no. 20 (May 22, 1915): 54.

38. "The Devil's Daughter," *Moving Picture World* 24, no. 13 (June 26, 1915): 2120.

CHAPTER 5. EGYPT ON THE GULF STREAM, 1915–1916

1. "Pauline Frederick Signs Long Contract," *Motion Picture News* 11, no. 22 (June 5, 1915): 40; *Bella Donna* Completed for Famous Players," *Moving Picture World* 26, no. 7 (November 6, 1915): 1159.

2. "Famous Players Company Here," *St. Augustine Record*, September 1, 1915, 1.

3. "Making the Movies," *St. Augustine Record*, September 4, 1915, 4; "Bella Donna," *Moving Picture World* 26, no. 8 (November 13, 1915): 1238.

4. *New York Times* excerpt quoted in "Tore Up Old City," *St. Augustine Record*, September 21, 1915, 1.

5. "Equitable Film Players Working," *St. Augustine Record*, October 9, 1915, 1; "Equitable Directors Afield," *Moving Picture World* 26, no. 5 (October 30, 1915): 802.

6. "Took Movies at Night," *St. Augustine Record*, December 2, 1915, 4; "Her Great Hour," *Motion Picture News* 13, no. 3 (January 22, 1916): 399.

7. "Movie Crowd Here," *St. Augustine Record*, November 6, 1915, 4; "Kalem Company Is Here," *St. Augustine Record*, November 13, 1915, 1; "Kalemites Here Again," *St. Augustine Record*, November 22, 1915, 4.

8. "Movie Company at Work," *St. Augustine Record*, December 15, 1915, 4; "The Lotus Woman," *Moving Picture World* 28, no. 10 (June 3, 1916): 1704; "The Lotus Woman," *Motion Picture News* 13, no. 24 (June 17, 1916): 3769.

9. "The Lotus Woman," *Moving Picture World* 28, no. 12 (June 17, 1916): 2055.

10. "Popular Film Company Here," *St. Augustine Record*, December 14, 1915, 8; "Her American Prince," *Moving Picture World* 29, no. 3 (July 15, 1916): 479.

11. "Hazel Dawn, Beautiful Screen Favorite," *St. Augustine Record*, December 10, 1915, 1; "Mrs. Dora Mills Adams," *St. Augustine Record*, December 18, 1915, 8; "My Lady Incog.," *Motion Picture News* 13, no. 4 (January 29, 1916): 558.

12. "My Lady Incog.," *Motography* 15, no. 5 (January 29, 1916): 267.

13. "At the Jefferson," *St. Augustine Record*, February 8, 1916, 5.

14. "Famous Players Coming," *St. Augustine Record*, December 16, 1915, 4; "The Spider," *Motion Picture News* 13, no. 4 (January 29, 1916): 453.

15. "Harry O. Hoyt with Metro," *Moving Picture World* 26, no. 13 (December 18, 1915): 2182; "Dimples," *Motography* 15, no. 9 (February 26, 1916): 485.

16. "Members of Metro Company Here," *St. Augustine Record*, January 22, 1916, 4; "A Corner in Cotton," *Motography* 15, no. 12 (March 18, 1916): 650.

17. "Invited Gaumont Company," *St. Augustine Record*, September 28, 1915, 4; "Gaumont Players Go South," *Moving Picture World* 26, no. 6 (October 30, 1915): 981; "Chamber of Commerce May Offer Inducements," *St. Augustine Record*, February 9, 1916, 1.

18. "Gaumont Motion Picture Co.," *St. Augustine Record*, January 4, 1916, 4; "The Dead Alive," *Motion Picture News* 13, no. 8 (February 26, 1916): 1138, 1178.

19. "Gaumont Co. Staging Picture," *St. Augustine Record*, February 9, 1916, 1; "The Haunted Manor," *Motion Picture News* 13, no. 9 (March 4, 1916): 1288.

20. "Southern Gaumont Companies," *Motion Picture News* 13, no. 8 (February 26, 1916): 1136.

21. "The Haunted Manor," *Motion Picture News* 13, no. 14 (April 8, 1916): 2067.

22. "Historic St. Augustine, Florida," *Moving Picture World* 28, no. 5 (April 29, 1916): 861.

23. "Pictures of Unveiling," *St. Augustine Record*, January 10, 1916, 4; "Showing Unveiling Movie," *St. Augustine Record*, March 10, 1916, 4.

24. "St. Augustine Has Everything," *St. Augustine Record*, January 20, 1916, 1; "St. Augustine Making Bid for Motion Picture Plants," *St. Augustine Record*, February 10, 1916, 4; "After Movie Companies," *St. Augustine Record*, June 1, 1916, 1.

25. "Ford Film Co. May Locate Here," *St. Augustine Record*, February 15, 1916, 1.

26. "Movie Company Here," *St. Augustine Record*, January 28, 1916, 1; "Movies at Orange Grove," *St. Augustine Record*, February 9, 1916, 4; "The Social Highwayman," *Motography* 15, no. 18 (April 29, 1916): 1000.

27. "Orpheum Theatre," *St. Augustine Record*, February 14, 1917, 5.

28. "An Interview with Edwin Thanhouser," *Reel Life*, October 23, 1915, 3, 16.

29. Bowers, *Thanhouser Films*, chap. 9; "Thanhouser Forces Gather in Jacksonville," *Motion Picture News* 13, no. 3 (January 22, 1916): 355; "The Oval Diamond," *Motion Picture News* 13, no. 8 (February 26, 1916): 1172.

30. "Prettiest Girl at the Ball," *Moving Picture World* 26, no. 13 (December 18, 1915): 2214; "What Doris Did," *Moving Picture World* 27, no. 11 (March 18, 1916): 1892; "Movie Company Here," *St. Augustine Record*, January 8, 1916, 4; "Orpheum Theatre," *St. Augustine Record*, May 3, 1916, 5.

31. "The Flight of the Duchess," *Motion Picture News* 13, no. 11 (March 18, 1916): 1616; "The Flight of the Duchess," *Motography* 15, no. 12 (March 18, 1916): 648; "Orpheum Theatre," *St. Augustine Record*, May 22, 1916, 5.

32. "Hidden Valley," *Motography* 16, no. 16 (October 14, 1916): 872; "Orpheum Theatre," *St. Augustine Record*, December 20, 1916, 5.

33. "The Image Maker," *Photo-Play Journal* 1, no. 10 (February 1917): 7–11; "Taking Motion Pictures," *St. Augustine Record*, May 5, 1916, 5; "Thanhouser Co. Working Here," *St. Augustine Record*, May 6, 1916, 5.

34. "Selig Co. Wants Local Actors," *St. Augustine Record*, March 29, 1916, 1, 7.

35. "Staging Great Picture Here," *St. Augustine Record*, March 30, 1916, 1; "Serial Film Company Much Pleased," *St. Augustine Record*, March 31, 1916, 1; "Wm. Steiner, Movie Manager, Coming," *St. Augustine Record*, April 18, 1916, 1; "The Yellow Menace," *Motion Picture News* 13, no. 23 (June 10, 1916): 3526.

36. Howells, "Confession of St. Augustine," 46.

37. "The Final Stand," *Moving Picture World* 31, no. 1 (January 6, 1917): 109.

38. Howells, "Confession of St. Augustine," 49.

39. "Vim Film Company Working Here," *St. Augustine Record*, April 14, 1916, 4; "Never Again," *Moving Picture World* 29, no. 1 (July 1, 1916): 136.

40. "Great Movie Campaign," *St. Augustine Record*, April 7, 1916, 1; "Record Movie Contest Is Great Advertising," *St. Augustine Record*, May 1, 1916, supplement; "Your Last Chance," *St. Augustine Record*, May 8, 1916, 3.

41. "Scenario Written by Miss Ida Lewis Floyd," *St. Augustine Record*, May 8, 1916, 1.

42. "Stage Struck Girls," *St. Augustine Record*, May 9, 1916, 8.

43. "Great Subscription Contest Is Over," *St. Augustine Record*, May 15, 1916, 1; "First Letter," *St. Augustine Record*, May 23, 1916, 8; "Movie Girl Contest," *St. Augustine Record*, May 25, 1916, 8; "Evening Record Party," *St. Augustine Record*, May 26, 1916, 8.

44. "Evening Record Party," *St. Augustine Record*, May 26, 1916, 8; "Each Succeeding Day," *St. Augustine Record*, May 29, 1916, 8; "First Day As Movie Stars," *St.*

Augustine Record, May 30, 1916, 8; "Stage Struck Girls," *St. Augustine Record*, May 31, 1916, 6; "Last Days in New York," *St. Augustine Record*, June 1, 1916, 8.

45. "Stage Struck Girls," *St. Augustine Record*, June 20, 1916, 5; "Stage Struck Girls Is Great," *St. Augustine Record*, June 21, 1916, 4; "Stage Struck Girls," *St. Augustine Record*, June 22, 1916, 5; "Philips-Oldfather," *St. Augustine Record*, November 16, 1917, 1.

46. "Motion Picture on Sunday," *St. Augustine Record*, June 23, 1916, 4; "Close Movies Sunday Nights," *St. Augustine Record*, June 23, 1916, 4.

47. Bean, *First Hollywood*, 97–99.

CHAPTER 6. LEADING LADIES TAKE CENTER STAGE, 1917

1. "More Movie Companies Coming to St. Augustine," *St. Augustine Record*, February 23, 1917, 1.

2. "Big Motion Picture Company Is Coming," *St. Augustine Record*, December 2, 1916, 1; "Motion Picture Company Arrives," *St. Augustine Record*, December 8, 1916, 5.

3. "The Eternal Sin," *Moving Picture World* 32, no. 1 (April 7, 1917): 108.

4. "Norma Talmadge Will Be in St. Augustine," *St. Augustine Record*, January 26, 1917, 1; "Norma Talmadge Here," *St. Augustine Record*, January 27, 1917, 2; "The Law of Compensation," *St. Augustine Record*, November 26, 1917, 3.

5. "Redemption," *Moving Picture World* 32, no. 9 (June 2, 1917): 1461.

6. "Redemption," Internet Movie Database, www.imdb.com; "Noted Movie Folks Coming," *St. Augustine Record*, January 26, 1917, 4.

7. "The Call of Her People," *Moving Picture World* 32, no. 11 (June 16, 1917): 1796.

8. "Ethel Barrymore Here," *St. Augustine Record*, January 16, 1917, 4; "New Ethel Barrymore Play," *Motography* 17, no. 18 (May 5, 1917): 957; "Early Silent Film Stars," *St. Augustine Record*, January 27, 1967, 2.

9. "Viola Dana Here," *St. Augustine Record*, February 22, 1917, 4; "'Lady Barnacle,' with Viola Dana, Completed," *Motion Picture News* 15, no. 14 (April 7, 1917): 2165; "Lady Barnacle," *Moving Picture World* 33, no. 3 (July 21, 1917): 474.

10. "Metro Stars Working Here," *St. Augustine Record*, February 9, 1917, 4; "Theater Parties Friday," *St. Augustine Record*, February 14, 1917, 4; "Miss Emmy Wehlen," *St. Augustine Record*, February 26, 1917, 1; "Metro Next Presents," *Motion Picture News* 15, no. 22 (June 2, 1917): 3431.

11. "Old-Time Actor Recalls," *St. Augustine Record*, February 26, 1917, 8.

12. "Moss Company in Florida," *Motography* 17, no. 5 (February 3, 1917): 261; "In the Hands of the Law," *Moving Picture World* 31, no. 7 (February 17, 1917): 972.

13. "Realism in 'In the Hands of the Law,'" *Moving Picture World* 31, no. 11 (March 17, 1917): 1788; "In the Hands of the Law," *Motography* 17, no. 11 (March 17, 1917): 568.

14. Petrova, *Butter*, 257.

15. Ibid., 273.

16. "Big Movie Stars Here," *St. Augustine Record*, January 20, 1917, 1; "Movie

Company Here," *St. Augustine Record*, January 23, 1917, 2; "To the Death," *Moving Picture World* 33, no. 12 (September 22, 1917): 1859.

17. "Madame Bernhardt Pleased," *St. Augustine Record*, January 17, 1917, 2.

18. Petrova, *Butter*, 281.

19. Ibid., 278.

20. "Mme. Petrova to Appear," *St. Augustine Record*, April 11, 1917, 8; "Madame Petrova," *St. Augustine Record*, April 13, 1917, 8.

21. "Olga Petrova Lasky Star," *Motography* 17, no. 1 (January 6, 1917): 20; "Madame Petrova Returning," *St. Augustine Record*, March 30, 1917, 4; "Mme. Olga Petrova Here," *St. Augustine Record*, April 2, 1917, 1.

22. "Movie Players at Work," *St. Augustine Record*, April 10, 1917, 4.

23. "Ovation Given Madam Petrova," *St. Augustine Record*, June 16, 1917, 4.

24. "The Undying Flame," *Motion Picture News* 15, no. 23 (June 9, 1917): 3619; "The Undying Flame," *Moving Picture World* 32, no. 10 (June 9, 1917): 1623; "The Undying Flame," *Motion Picture Magazine* 14, no. 7 (August 1917): 7.

25. Petrova, *Butter*, 282.

26. "St. Augustine Notes," *Florida Times-Union*, April 11, 1917, 2; "Building Movie Huts," *St. Augustine Record*, April 16, 1917, 4; "Lasky Players at Work," *St. Augustine Record*, April 18, 1917, 2; "Movie Players at Work," *Florida Times-Union*, April 19, 1917, 7; "Local People in Petrova Picture," *St. Augustine Record*, April 19, 1917, 2; "Hundreds in Movies Today," *St. Augustine Record*, April 21, 1917, 4.

27. "Children in the Movies," *St. Augustine Record*, April 19, 1917, 2.

28. "At the Jefferson," *St. Augustine Record*, October 1, 1917, 3; "Exile," *Moving Picture World* 34, no. 1 (October 6, 1917): 71.

29. "The Law of the Land," *Moving Picture World* 33, no. 9 (September 1, 1917): 1385; "Jefferson Ready," *St. Augustine Record*, September 8, 1917, 1.

30. "Taking Pictures for Movies," *St. Augustine Record*, January 12, 1917, 4; "Players Escape to Florida," *Motography* 17, no. 6 (February 10, 1917): 305.

31. "Miss Doro Here," *St. Augustine Record*, February 27, 1917, 8; "Paramount Players Here," *St. Augustine Record*, March 1, 1917, 2; "Famous Players at Work," *St. Augustine Record*, March 7, 1917, 4; "Famous Players Actors," *St. Augustine Record*, March 8, 1917, 1; "Took Night Pictures," *St. Augustine Record*, March 8, 1917, 4; "The Eastern Studios," *Motion Picture News* 15, no. 2 (March 24, 1917): 1835; "News of the Film World," *Variety* 46, no. 5 (March 30, 1917): 23.

32. "Posed for Camera," *St. Augustine Record*, March 6, 1917, 4.

33. "Fox Film Company," *St. Augustine Record*, February 2, 1917, 2; "Theda Bara Coming," *St. Augustine Record*, February 3, 1917, 4.

34. "Fox Film Company Stars," *St. Augustine Record*, February 7, 1917, 1; "Theda Bara, World Famous Screen Star," *St. Augustine Record*, February 9, 1917, 1; "Theda Bara Has Arrived," *St. Augustine Record*, February 9, 1917, 1; "Silent Movies in St. Augustine," *St. Augustine Record*, March 27, 1951, 8.

35. "Movie Star to Plant Palm Tree," *St. Augustine Record*, February 13, 1917, 1; "Many Hundreds Saw Miss Bara," *St. Augustine Record*, February 19, 1917, 1; "Miss Theda Bara Planting a Date Palm," *St. Augustine Record*, February 20, 1917, 6; "Former Resident, Now in California, Writes," *St. Augustine Record*, April 11, 1951, 2.

36. "Showed Local Picture," *St. Augustine Record*, March 16, 1917, 4; "Miss Bara Presents Picture of Tree Planting to City," *St. Augustine Record*, March 21, 1917, 4.

37. W. Livingston Larned, "Penned at Random," *St. Augustine Record*, March 22, 1917, 2.

38. "Sick Were Given Wedding Flowers," *St. Augustine Record*, February 22, 1917, 3.

39. "At the Orpheum," *St. Augustine Record*, May 4, 1917, 5; "Early Silent Movie Stars," *St. Augustine Record*, January 22, 1967, 2.

40. "Theda Falls Near Big Alligator," *St. Augustine Record*, May 9, 1917, 3.

41. "Narrowly Escapes Accident," *St. Augustine Record*, February 12, 1917, 4.

42. "Fox Film Co. Build Great Setting," *St. Augustine Record*, February 27, 1917, 4; "Movie People Working," *St. Augustine Record*, March 17, 1917; W. Livingston Larned, "Penned at Random," *St. Augustine Record*, March 22, 1917, 2.

43. "Fire Threatened Movie Place," *St. Augustine Record*, March 8, 1917, 4; "Fox Film Co. Completes Work," *St. Augustine Record*, March 28, 1917, 1.

44. "Heart and Soul," *Motography* 17, no. 22 (June 2, 1917): 1176; "Heart and Soul," *Moving Picture World* 32, no. 10 (June 9, 1917): 1622; "Heart and Soul," *Motion Picture Magazine* 14, no. 7 (August 1917): 10; "She Made Suicide Scene," *St. Augustine Record*, February 5, 1967, 12.

45. "Heart and Soul," *Motography* 17, no. 22 (June 2, 1917): 1176.

46. "Orpheum Theatre," *St. Augustine Record*, June 14, 1917, 5; "Automobile Procession," *St. Augustine Record*, June 16, 1917, 5; "More Enthusiastic Crowds," *St. Augustine Record*, June 18, 1917, 2.

47. "Bara Attends Movies," *St. Augustine Record*, March 19, 1917, 4.

48. "An 'Off' to the Rays," *Variety* 20, no. 5 (October 8, 1910): 6; "Johnny and Emma Ray," *Variety* 22, no. 8 (April 29, 1911): 21; "The Jefferson Theatre," *St. Augustine Record*, April 8, 1912, 1.

49. "Ray Comedies," *Moving Picture World* 28, no. 8 (May 20, 1916): 1344; "Four Johnnie Ray Comedies," *Moving Picture World* 28, no. 9 (May 27, 1916): 1534; "The Ray Comedies," *Motion Picture News* 13, no. 22 (June 3, 1916): 3430; "Johnny and Emma Ray," *St. Augustine Record*, July 11, 1916, 5.

50. "Mr. and Mrs. Ray Here," *St. Augustine Record*, February 14, 1917, 4; "Johnny Ray to Establish Movie Industry Here," *St. Augustine Record*, February 15, 1917, 1; "C. of C. Takes Action," *St. Augustine Record*, February 16, 1917, 1; "Johnny Ray Company," *St. Augustine Record*, March 6, 1917, 1; "Movie Company Working," *St. Augustine Record*, March 9, 1917, 6; "Enjoying Movies," *St. Augustine Record*, March 10, 1917, 4; "John Ray Goes North," *St. Augustine Record*, March 22, 1917, 4; Bean, *First Hollywood*, 102.

51. "Johnny and Emma Ray in Movies," *Moving Picture World* 32, no. 10 (June 9, 1917): 1638; "Ray Comedies," *Moving Picture World* 32, no. 12 (June 23, 1917): 1907; "At the Orpheum," *St. Augustine Record*, October 4, 1917, 3.

52. "Famous Emma Ray," *Hollywood Filmograph* 13, no. 40 (October 14, 1933): 1.

53. "Many Brilliant Stars Here," *St. Augustine Record*, March 27, 1917, 1; "Ivan Film Company Left Friday," *St. Augustine Record*, March 31, 1917, 10.

54. "August's New Color Idea," *New York Clipper* 65, no. 4 (February 28, 1917): 34; "New Art Co. Goes South," *Variety* 46, no. 2 (March 9, 1917): 18; "Edwin August Busy," *Variety* 46, no. 11 (May 11, 1917): 21.

55. "Motion-Picture Company Coming," *St. Augustine Record*, May 17, 1917, 4; "Edwin August Heads Studio," *St. Augustine Record*, May 19, 1917, 4; "Movie Actors Here," *St. Augustine Record*, June 1, 1917, 4.

56. "Famous Players Company," *St. Augustine Record*, July 16, 1917, 1; "Famous Players Company Left," *St. Augustine Record*, July 18, 1917, 1; "Barbary Sheep," *Motography* 18, no. 14 (December 6, 1917): 737.

CHAPTER 7. WARTIME CONDITIONS, 1917–1918

1. "Mary Garden Here," *St. Augustine Record*, October 10, 1917, 1; "Lost in the Wilds," *St. Augustine Record*, October 11, 1917, 4; "Back to New York," *St. Augustine Record*, October 12, 1917, 4; "Mary Garden Returns from Florida," *Moving Picture World* 34, no. 6 (November 10, 1917): 892.

2. "Thais," *Motion Picture News* 17, no. 4 (January 26, 1918): 594–95; "Thais," *Motography* 19, no. 4 (January 26, 1918): 179; "Mary Garden in 'Thais,'" *Picture-Play Magazine* 8, no. 1 (March 1918): 104–5; "Comments and Criticisms," *Film Fun* 348 (March–April 1918): 7–9.

3. "Nazimova Is Sponsor," *Motography* 18, no. 19 (November 10, 1917): 980; "Nazimova Is Coming," *St. Augustine Record*, December 8, 1917, 1; "Jefferson Theatre," *St. Augustine Record*, January 24, 1919, 3.

4. "Newslets for Use," *Motography* 19, no. 4 (January 26, 1918): 192; "Fate Decider," *Moving Picture World* 36, no. 3 (April 20, 1918): 405; "Toys of Fate," *Motion Picture News* 17, no. 21 (May 25, 1918): 3047.

5. "Famous Players Here," *St. Augustine Record*, November 12, 1917, 1; "Madame Jealousy," *Motography* 19, no. 7 (February 16, 1918): 324.

6. "Pauline Frederick Here," *St. Augustine Record*, December 3, 1917, 1; "Movie People in Accident," *St. Augustine Record*, December 5, 1917, 4; "Famous Players Attend Matinee," *St. Augustine Record*, December 7, 1917, 2.

7. "Many Saw Exciting Scene," *St. Augustine Record*, December 6, 1917, 4; "Another Atrocity," *St. Augustine Record*, December 7, 1917, 2; "La Tosca," *Moving Picture World* 35, no. 4 (January 26, 1918): 544; "Former Resident," *St. Augustine Record*, April 11, 1951, 4.

8. "Famous Players Finish Here," *St. Augustine Record*, December 13, 1917, 8; "Miss Frederick Finished 'La Tosca,'" *Motography* 19, no. 7 (February 16, 1918): 322; "Green Room Jottings," *Motion Picture Magazine* 15, no. 2 (March 1918): 112.

9. Petrova, *Butter*, 283–84.

10. Ibid., 285; "Madame Petrova Coming," *St. Augustine Record*, December 14, 1917, 2; "Daughter of Destiny," *Moving Picture World* 35, no. 3 (January 19, 1918): 378; "Jefferson Theatre," *St. Augustine Record*, June 1, 1918, 3.

11. Petrova, *Butter*, 284ff.

12. "Motion Picture Theaters," *St. Augustine Record*, October 29, 1917, 1; "Take Pennies to Movies," *St. Augustine Record*, October 31, 1917, 1.

13. "City Booking and Filling Many Orders," *St. Augustine Record*, January 5, 1918, 1; "City Supplying Fuel," *St. Augustine Record*, January 17, 1918, 4.

14. "Fuel Restrictions Affect St. Augustine," *St. Augustine Record*, January 18, 1918, 1; "Heatless Monday Observed Here," *St. Augustine Record*, January 22, 1918, 1; "Business as Usual," *St. Augustine Record*, February 9, 1918, 1; "Exit Heatless Monday," *Moving Picture World* 35, no. 9 (March 2, 1918): 1204.

15. "War Curtails Picture Production," *Motography* 19, no. 5 (February 2, 1918): 213.

16. "Colored People Admitted," *St. Augustine Record*, June 19, 1918, 4.

17. "Lincolnville Theater Opens," *St. Augustine Record*, August 13, 1918, 4.

18. "Miss Billie Burke at Ponce de Leon," *St. Augustine Record*, February 11, 1918, 4; "Let's Get a Divorce," *Moving Picture World* 35, no. 11 (March 16, 1918): 1534.

19. "Let's Get a Divorce," *Motography* 19, no. 12 (March 23, 1918): 576; "Let's Get a Divorce," *Moving Picture World* 36, no. 5 (May 4, 1918): 744; "Let's Get a Divorce," *Picture-Play Magazine* 8, no. 4 (June 1918): 280–89.

20. "Death Takes Two Prominent Men," *Motography* 19, no. 7 (February 16, 1918): 304; "Drastic Steps Taken," *St. Augustine Record*, October 7, 1918, 4.

21. "Company Here," *St. Augustine Record*, March 9, 1918, 1.

22. "Local News," *St. Augustine Record*, March 13, 1918, clipping, Silent Films file, St. Augustine Historical Society; "Vengeance," *Motion Picture News* 17, no. 21 (May 25, 1918): 3142; "Big Feature Picture," *St. Augustine Record*, June 6, 1918, 4.

23. "Jefferson Theatre Opens Today," *St. Augustine Record*, November 1, 1918, 4; "Orpheum Renovated," *St. Augustine Record*, November 1, 1918, 4; "Blaze at the Jefferson," *St. Augustine Record*, November 11, 1918, 4.

24. "Orpheum Theatre Temporarily Closed," *St. Augustine Record*, October 2, 1919, 8; "Lynch Enterprises Expanding," *St. Augustine Record*, November 14, 1919, 4.

CHAPTER 8. INTO THE SUNSET, 1919 TO "THE END"

1. "Motion Picture Folk Beginning to Arrive," *St. Augustine Record*, January 8, 1919, 1; "Florida for the Movies," *St. Augustine Record*, January 10, 1919, 2.

2. Bean, *First Hollywood*, 102–3.

3. "Here to Produce Moving Pictures," *St. Augustine Record*, January 10, 1919, 1; "Noted Star Saw Her Own Picture," *St. Augustine Record*, January 13, 1919, 4; "Made in St. Augustine," *St. Augustine Record*, May 10, 1919, 4; "Three Green Eyes," *Moving Picture World* 40, no. 4 (April 26, 1919): 573.

4. "Moving Picture Stars Coming," *St. Augustine Record*, January 29, 1920, 4; "Ft. Marion to Figure In," *St. Augustine Record*, January 30, 1920, 1; "Motion Picture Players Think This Is Venice," *St. Augustine Record*, February 2, 1920, 1; "Rainfall Total 14.65 Inches," *St. Augustine Record*, February 2, 1920, 1.

5. "Cosmopolitan Actors Perform," *St. Augustine Record*, February 2, 1920, 4.

6. "Returned to New York," *St. Augustine Record*, February 14, 1920, 4; "The World and His Wife," *Motion Picture News* 22, no. 6 (July 31, 1920): 1003; "At the Jefferson," *St. Augustine Record*, August 14, 1920, 3; "St. Augustine Scenes Were Beautiful," *St. Augustine Record*, August 16, 1920, 4.

7. "Frohman Serial Is Completed," *Motion Picture News* 21 (May 15, 1920): 4177.

8. "Motion Picture Company Is Here," *St. Augustine Record*, April 26, 1920, 1; "Former Visitor with Motion Picture Company," *St. Augustine Record*, April 27, 1920, 4.

9. "Working at the Hotel Ponce de Leon," *St. Augustine Record*, April 27, 1920, 4; "Oriental Settings," *St. Augustine Record*, April 29, 1920, 4; "Delighted with St. Augustine," *St. Augustine Record*, May 1, 1920, 4.

10. "Vitagraph Co. Sends Group," *St. Augustine Record*, May 12, 1920, 1; "Watching the Movies," *St. Augustine Record*, May 13, 1920, 4; "An Interesting Scene," *St. Augustine Record*, May 14, 1920, 4.

11. "The Whisper Market," *Wid's Daily* 13, no. 59 (August 29, 1920): 15.

12. "What Does It Cost?" *Motion Picture Magazine* 31, no. 6 (July 1926): 20–21; "William Fox Builds," *Motion Picture News* 19, no. 23 (June 7, 1919): 3771–72.

13. "Experience Doing Good," *Variety* 62, no. 3 (March 4, 1921): 35; "Special Cast in Experience," *Exhibitor's Herald* 63, no. 10 (September 3, 1921): 57; "Scenes Made Here," *St. Augustine Record*, December 13, 1921, 4.

14. "Motion Pictures in the Making," *St. Augustine Record*, April 1, 1922, 4.

15. "Movie Company Is in City," *St. Augustine Record*, April 3, 1922, 1; "Picture Company Start to Work," *St. Augustine Record*, April 5, 1922, 4.

16. "Speed," *Film Daily* 21, no. 70 (September 10, 1922): 15; "Pathé Will Release 'Speed,'" *Exhibitor's Trade Review* 12, no. 18 (September 30, 1922): 1180.

17. "Artists of Silver Screen," *St. Augustine Record*, January 19, 1923, 4; "Motion Picture Players at Fort," *St. Augustine Record*, January 20, 1923, 1; "Burr Unit Goes South," *Exhibitor's Trade Review* 13, no. 10 (February 3, 1923): 500; "Studio and Players Brevities," *Motion Picture News* 27, no. 7 (February 17, 1923): 868; "Burr Comedies," *Motion Picture News* 27, no. 12 (March 24, 1923): 1467; "Scenes for Comedy," *St. Augustine Record*, May 23, 1923, 8.

18. "The Confidence Man," *St. Augustine Record*, January 24, 1924, 4.

19. "Favorite Star of Filmdom Is Guest at Hotel Alcazar," *St. Augustine Record*, January 11, 1924, 1; "Star Consents to Appear," *St. Augustine Record*, January 12, 1924, 1; "Public Appearance of Thomas Meighan," *St. Augustine Record*, January 14, 1924, 1.

20. "Poor House Scenes," *St. Augustine Record*, January 21, 1924, 1.

21. "Work Comes First with Thomas Meighan," *St. Augustine Record*, January 15, 1924, 8; "Coming to See 'The Confidence Man,'" *St. Augustine Record*, April 20, 1924, 4.

22. "Leading Lady," *St. Augustine Record*, January 12, 1924, 4; "Unusual Scene in 'Quicksands,'" *St. Augustine Record*, January 16, 1924, 1; "Crowd Saw Taking of Meighan Picture," *St. Augustine Record*, January 23, 1924, 4.

23. "St. Augustine to Have First Showing," *St. Augustine Record*, April 17, 1924, 3; "Coming to See 'The Confidence Man,'" *St. Augustine Record*, April 20, 1924, 4.

24. "To Film Scenes in 'White Mice,'" *St. Augustine Record*, December 17, 1924, 5.

25. "Would You Like to See Your Girl Friend in the Movies?" *St. Augustine Record*, April 23, 1925, 3; "St. Augustine to Be Featured in Interesting Movie," *St. Augustine Record*, April 24, 1925, 3; "Movie Scenes Will Be Taken Here," *St. Augustine Record*, April 25, 1925, 3.

26. "Agnes Carrera Is Chosen As Star," *St. Augustine Record*, May 1, 1925, 1; "Moving Pictures Being Taken in St. Augustine," *St. Augustine Record*, May 2, 1925, 4.

27. "St. Augustine Girl in Leading Role," *St. Augustine Record*, May 12, 1925, 3; "The Trickster's Fate," *St. Augustine Record*, May 13, 1925, 3; "Local Moving Picture at Jefferson," *St. Augustine Record*, May 14, 1925, 4.

28. "Famous Melody Series," *Motion Picture News* 33, no. 6 (February 6, 1926): 690; "In Eastern Studios," *Film Daily* 36, no. 3 (April 4, 1926): 10.

29. "Interest Is Added to Tea," *St. Augustine Record*, March 12, 1926, 2; "Songs of Spain," *St. Augustine Record*, March 12, 1926, 8; "Songs of Old Spain," *St. Augustine Record*, March 16, 1926, 8.

BIBLIOGRAPHY

NEWSPAPERS AND PERIODICALS

Cinema
Exhibitor's Herald
Exhibitor's Trade Review
Film Daily
Film Fun
Hollywood Filmograph
(Jacksonville) Florida Times-Union
Kinetogram
Motion Picture Magazine
Motion Picture News
Motography
Movie Pictorial
Moving Picture News
Moving Picture World
New York Clipper
Photofest
Photoplay
Photo-Play Journal
Picture-Play Magazine
Picture Play Weekly
Reel Life
St. Augustine Evening Record
St. Augustine Record
The Tatler (St. Augustine)
Variety
Wid's Daily

Bean, Jennifer M., and Diana Negra. "The Queer Career of Jim Crow." In *A Feminist Reader in Early Cinema*, ed. Siobhan B. Somerville. Durham, NC: Duke University Press, 2002.

Bean, Shawn C. *The First Hollywood: Florida and the Golden Age of Silent Filmmaking.* Gainesville: University Press of Florida, 2008.

Bowers, Q. David. *Thanhouser Films: An Encyclopedia and History.* Thanhouser Company Film Preservation. www.thanhouser.org/tcocd/

Brasell, R. Bruce. "A Seed for Change: The Engenderment of *A Florida Enchantment*." *Cinema Journal* 36, no. 4 (Summer 1997): 3–21.

Eckhardt, Joseph P. *The King of the Movies: Film Pioneer Siegmund Lubin.* Cranbury, NJ: Associated University Presses, 1997.

Everson, William K. *American Silent Film.* New York: Oxford University Press, 1978.

Gauntier, Gene. "Blazing the Trail." *Women's Home Companion*, November 1928, 15–16, 132, 134.

Goddard, Charles. *The Perils of Pauline: A Motion Picture Novel.* New York: Hearst's International Library, 1915.

Hope, Laura Lee. *The Moving Picture Girls: Under the Palms.* New York: Grosset & Dunlap, 1914.

Howells, William Dean. "A Confession of St. Augustine." *El Escribano* (St. Augustine Historical Society) 35 (1998): 33–60. Originally published in *Harper's Monthly Magazine*, April and May 1917.

Media History Digital Library: A Resource for Film, TV, and Radio History, mediahistoryproject.org.

Miller, Blair. *Almost Hollywood: The Forgotten Story of Jacksonville, Florida.* Lanham, MD: Hamilton Books, 2013.

Mix, Paul E. *Tom Mix: A Heavily Illustrated Biography.* Jefferson, NC: McFarland, 1995.

Newton, Michael. *Lights! Camera! Florida! Ninety Years of Moviemaking and Television Production in the Sunshine State.* Tampa: Florida Endowment for the Humanities, 1987.

Petrova, Olga. *Butter for My Bread.* New York: Bobbs-Merrill, 1942.

Sargent, Epes Winthrop. *Techniques of the Photoplay.* New York: Moving Picture World, 1913.

Smith, Albert E. *Two Reels and a Crank.* Garden City, NY: Doubleday, 1952.

Waldman, Harry. *Maurice Tourneur: The Life and Films.* Jefferson, NC: McFarland, 2001.

Waterbury, Jean Parker, ed. *The Oldest City: St. Augustine Saga of Survival.* St. Augustine, FL: St. Augustine Historical Society, 1983.

INDEX

Thomas Graham is professor of history emeritus, Flagler College, and lives in St. Augustine, Florida. He is the author of *Mr. Flagler's St. Augustine*.